CorelDRAW

A Visual Approach for the Beginner

Welcome to **Quick & Easy.** Designed for the true novice, this new series covers basic tasks in a simple, learn-by-doing fashion. If that sounds like old news to you, take a closer look.

Quick & Easy books are a bit like picture books. They're for people who would rather see and do than read and ponder. The books are colorful. They're full of illustrations, and accompanying text that is straightforward, concise, and easy to read.

But don't waste your time reading about our **Quick & Easy** books; start learning your new software package, instead. This **Quick & Easy** book is just the place to start.

CorelDRAW
Quick & Easy

Robin Merrin

SYBEX®

San Francisco • Paris • Düsseldorf • Soest

Acquisitions Editor: David Clark
Series Editor: Christian T. S. Crumlish
Developmental Editor: Kenyon Brown
Editor: Savitha Varadan
Technical Editor: Maryann Brown
Series Designers: Helen Bruno, Ingrid Owen
Production Artist: Alissa Feinberg
Desktop Publishing Specialist: Suzanne Albertson
Proofreader/Production Assistant: Rhonda Holmes
Indexer: Ted Laux
Cover Illustrator: Richard Miller
Cover Designer: Archer Design

Library of Congress Card Number: 92-62082
ISBN: 0-7821-1194-7

Manufactured in the United States of America
10 9 8 7 6 5 4 3 2 1

ACKNOWLEDGMENTS

●

I would like to thank my sister, Deane Swick, an accomplished graphic designer, painter, art teacher, and computer graphics instructor for finding the time to create original designs in CorelDRAW and CorelPHOTO-PAINT to be used in the lessons. Her insight into the way a graphic professional would want to use CorelDRAW was also a tremendous help. I'd also like to apologize to her for the small changes I made to her designs. My only defense is that I usually wanted to give you, the reader, an opportunity to try one more tool or option.

I'm equally indebted to my husband, business partner, and technical expert, Thomas Merrin, for helping to plan and then test the lessons to make sure they worked, suggesting improvements along the way, and also for capturing every screen.

Finally, I'd like to thank Dianne King and David Clark at SYBEX for asking me to write this book, Savitha Varadan for editing it, and Mary-ann Brown for providing the careful technical edits.

Contents
at a Glance

Contents

Quick&Easy

If you'd like someone to teach you to use CorelDRAW, but there isn't anyone you can ask, then this book is for you. The Corel Graphics applications offer an enormous number of features and capabilities. As a result, you'll probably wonder how best to begin working in each application and quickly see results. You'll find the answer here. In ten easy lessons, you'll learn to use not only CorelDRAW, but all the other main applications that are included in the box: CorelMOSAIC, CorelPHOTO-PAINT, CorelSHOW, and CorelCHART. You'll also find out how to import and modify the clip art images, symbols, and fonts to create professional-looking designs, drawings, and charts right away—even if you aren't a graphic design professional.

This book is designed as a tutorial, which means you'll learn by doing. You'll draw freehand and with drawing tools. You'll create interesting effects with CorelDRAW's text-handling capabilities. You'll create charts by modifying some data and then clicking on a picture of a chart. You'll enhance an image with painting tools—CorelPHOTO-PAINT tools that provide different capabilities from the drawing tools in CorelDRAW. And, you'll pull together drawings, charts, and animations to develop an on-screen demonstration of your capabilities.

Hardware and Software Requirements

If you are considering the purchase of CorelDRAW, make sure your equipment meets these requirements. You must have:

- A 100% IBM-PC compatible computer with either a 386-based or 486-based CPU, or a 286-based CPU with adequate memory to run Windows in Standard mode.

- At least 2 MB of RAM; however, 4 MB or 8 MB of RAM is strongly recommended so that you can work at a productive pace.

- Windows 3.0 or 3.1.

- A minimum of 11 to 12 MB of free disk space to install only CorelDRAW; or a maximum of 34 MB of free disk space to install all the applications, samples, fonts, and symbols.

- A VGA color or monochrome monitor or better (for example, a super-VGA monitor) that is compatible with the version of Windows you are running. Since you'll be working with graphics, color is strongly recommended.

- A mouse or other pointing device (for example, a mouse pen or trackball) that is compatible with Windows.

You'll probably find it is worthwhile to invest in any hardware and software you lack so you can work with CorelDRAW. It's the most powerful graphic illustration package on the market.

How This Book Is Organized

This book is divided into two parts. Part One is devoted almost entirely to the drawing application CorelDRAW, as it remains the most important component, and probably the reason you bought the product. No matter how little computer experience or graphic design knowledge you have, you can become reasonably adept at using CorelDRAW productively with a few lessons that help you sort out the basics. You'll become skilled at creating drawings and business documents with original art, clip art, and CorelDRAW symbols. You'll also learn how to use the file manager CorelMOSAIC to browse through and open files. This saves time when you're looking for a file or a clip art image.

In Part Two, you'll discover how to use the other major applications that are included in the package. You'll have an opportunity to enhance a drawing or other image with CorelPHOTO-PAINT. You'll create and produce an on-screen presentation with CorelSHOW, including some images from CorelDRAW and CorelCHART in the show. Finally, you'll become familiar with CorelCHART's templates and samples, automatically generating and then enhancing charts of your own.

You do not have to proceed through all the lessons in order; you can skip lessons that do not interest you at the moment and choose what you need to accomplish right away. Once you've installed CorelDRAW in Lesson 1, we suggest you proceed through Lessons 2, 3, and 4, to give you a solid foundation in using the tools. Then you can select the lessons that can help you complete any pressing business tasks. Later, you can return to other lessons, as time permits.

Learning to Use CorelDRAW

Part One is entirely devoted to CorelDRAW itself, as the drawing application remains the most important component of the package, and is probably the reason you invested in it.

Whether you are a professional artist or a non-artistic business user, you can become reasonably adept at using CorelDRAW productively with a few lessons that help you sort out the basics. In Part One, you'll learn to create drawings and business documents with original art and clip art, and use your art in other documents, such as brochures and newsletters.

Installing CorelDRAW

1

Lesson 1 tells you how to install CorelDRAW and, if you wish, the other Corel applications from the Setup disks included in the CorelDRAW package. These are the other applications that you can also install:

- CorelTRACE

- CorelCHART

- CorelPHOTO-PAINT

- CorelSHOW

- CorelMOSAIC

- Fonts & Symbols

Installation Requirements

CorelDRAW requires the following to run:

- A 100% IBM-PC compatible computer with either a 386-based or 486-based CPU, or a 286-based CPU with adequate memory to run Windows in Standard mode.

- At least 2 MB of RAM.

- Windows 3.0 or 3.1.

- A minimum of 11 to 12 MB of free disk space to install only CorelDRAW. A maximum of 29 MB of free disk space to install all the applications, samples, fonts, and symbols when installing under Windows 3.1, or 30 Mb of free disk space when installing under Windows 3.0.

- A VGA color or monochrome monitor or better (for example, a super-VGA monitor), that is compatible with the version of Windows you are running. Since you'll be working with graphics, color is strongly recommended.

- A mouse or other pointing device (for example, a mouse pen) that is compatible with Windows.

Windows 3.0 or Windows 3.1?

There are two significant differences in the capabilities you'll have when running CorelDRAW under Windows 3.0 or 3.1, and because of those differences, Windows 3.1 is strongly recommended. However, if you currently have Windows 3.0 installed, you do not have to wait until you upgrade to Windows 3.1. Go ahead and install CorelDRAW today and begin working with it. Just be aware of the differences as you begin working:

- Although you can run CorelDRAW under Windows 3.0, you will not be able to use the TrueType fonts which are installed with CorelDRAW. You will need either the Corel WFN fonts from an earlier version of CorelDRAW or Adobe Type Manager. And, you will not be able to use Adobe Type 1 fonts either unless you have a CD-ROM drive; the Adobe fonts are on the CD-ROM disk included with CorelDRAW 3.0.

- The applications that are included with Windows 3.0, such as Paintbrush and Write are not OLE-capable, as are the applications included with Windows 3.1. *OLE* stands for object linking and embedding, and it lets you share information between applications.

Whether you are a graphic designer or a business user creating illustrations for your presentations, the type limitations will probably motivate you to upgrade to Windows 3.1. The differences in information sharing, on the other hand, will probably be less important to you in your early work.

Freeing Enough Disk Space

When you begin the installation process, CorelDRAW will check to make sure you have adequate hard disk space before you begin. You will not be able to start installing unless you have enough free disk space. However, you'll save some time if you check this yourself first and, if necessary, delete or move some files to floppy disks.

You can use the File Manager in Windows to do this. Refer to the *Microsoft Windows User's Guide* for more information.

Running Setup

The installation process is driven by the Windows Setup program. You can decide to do a either a full or custom installation. The steps are the same whether you are installing CorelDRAW under Windows 3.0 or 3.1. Begin from the Program Manager in Windows.

1. From the DOS prompt, type **WIN** and press ↵.

2. Pull down the File menu and choose Run. To pull down the menu, point to File with the mouse pointer and click the left mouse button. To choose Run, point to it with

Click here to open the File menu.

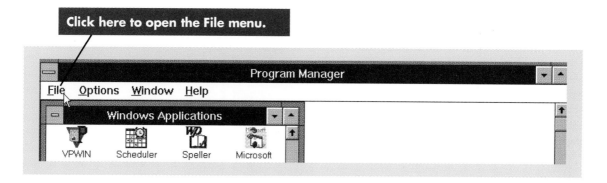

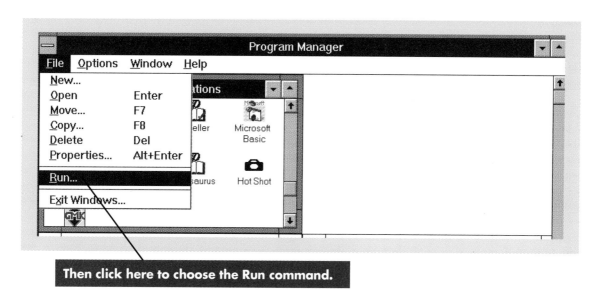

Then click here to choose the Run command.

the mouse pointer and click the left mouse button.

3. Insert Disk #1 in either disk drive and then type **A:SETUP** or **B:SETUP** (depending on the drive where you inserted the disk) in the Command Line box. To type in this box, first point to the box with your mouse and then click in it. Then type the text at the keyboard.

Quick **Easy**

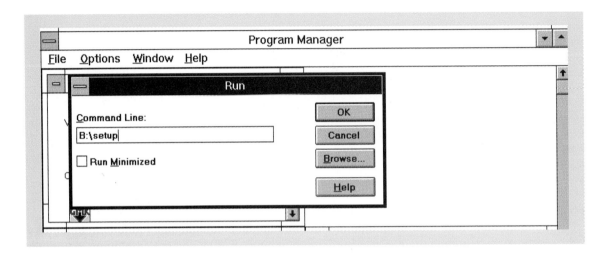

4. Press ↵ or click OK.

First, you'll see the CorelDRAW Setup box which displays "Initializing Setup, one moment please."

This is followed by the CorelDRAW 3.0 Setup dialog box.

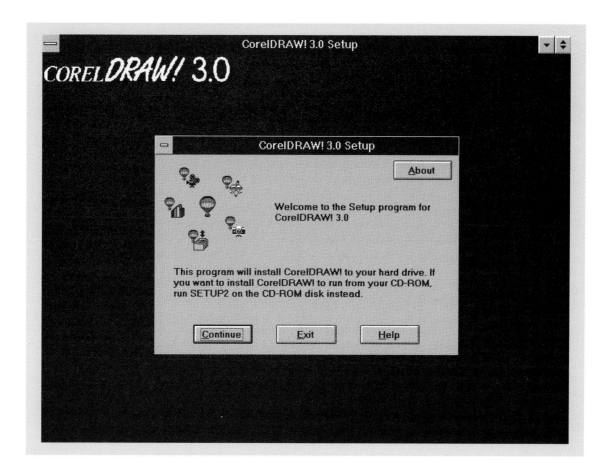

5. Choose Continue.

Now, you'll see the CorelDRAW Installation Options dialog box with three options from which you should choose:

- Full Install

- Minimum Install

- Custom Install

Quick & Easy

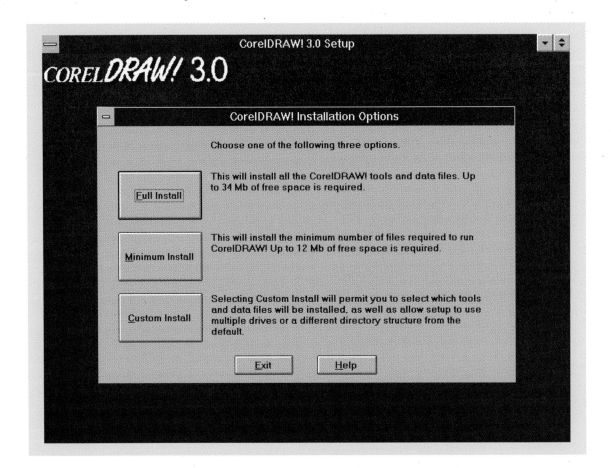

To select any option in any of the Setup dialog boxes, you can click on the button or option, or press ↑, ↓, or Tab to move to the option and then press ↵.

If you want to install all the Corel applications, continue to the next section, "Running a Full Installation." If you want to install the minimum amount of files needed to run just CorelDRAW, continue to the section, "Running a Minimum Installation." If you want to install only some of the applications, sample files, and fonts and symbols, but more than the minimum, skip ahead to "Running a Custom Installation."

Running a Full Installation

1. To install all the applications, click on Full Install.

The Set Destination Path dialog box is displayed. It shows
C:\CORELDRW as the drive and directory where CorelDRAW will be
installed, unless you decide to install it at another location.

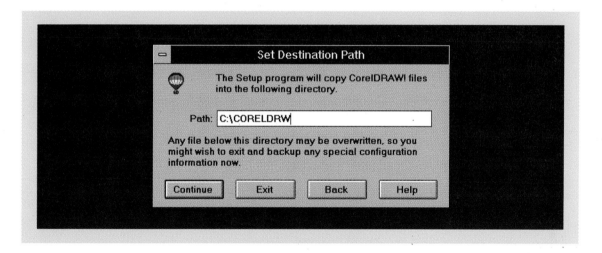

2. If you have sufficient free disk space on your C drive, click
Continue. If you need to install CorelDRAW on a different
drive, change the drive letter. Click in the Path text box to
place the cursor before the C, press **Del**, then type **D** (or
any other drive letter). Then choose Continue.

CorelDRAW then checks the drive to make sure you have enough free
disk space. This takes a few minutes on most computers. When it is finished checking, you'll see the CorelDRAW Setup Disk 1 progress box.
The information in this box changes as the installation proceeds. If you
need to stop the installation process at any time, simply click the Cancel button.

When all the files from Setup Disk 1 have been copied, you'll see the message "Please insert the diskette labeled CorelDRAW Setup disk 2 in A:" (or B: if you began the installation from B:).

3. Remove Setup Disk 1 and insert Setup Disk 2, then click OK.

4. Continue inserting the next disk in order each time you see the message requesting another disk.

When you have inserted the last Setup disk, skip to the section "When Installation is Complete" at the end of this lesson.

Running a Minimum Installation

1. To install only the minimum files needed to run Corel-DRAW, click on Minimum. Then follow the steps in the previous section, "Running a Full Installation."

The only difference you'll notice during the process is that Corel-DRAW will not ask you to insert all the Setup disks, because it will not be installing all the files.

Running a Custom Installation

1. To install the applications, samples, and symbols and fonts of your choice, click on Custom Install.

The Set Destination Path dialog box is displayed. It shows the drive and directory where CorelDRAW will be installed, unless you decide to install it at another location.

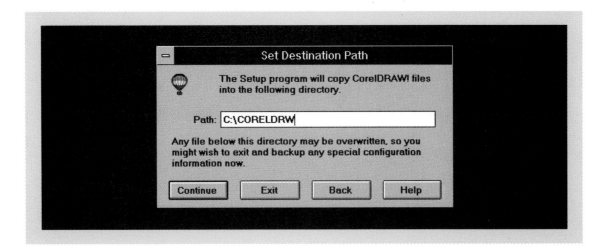

Quick & Easy

2. If you have sufficient free disk space on your C drive, click
Continue. If you need to install CorelDRAW on a different
drive, change the drive letter. Click in the text box to place
the cursor before the C, press **Del**, then type **D** (or any other
drive letter). Then choose Continue.

CorelDRAW then checks the drive to make sure you have enough free
disk space. When it is finished checking, the custom installation dialog
box is displayed.

					Disk Usage:
CorelDRAW!:		●		C:\CORELDRW\DRAW\	6738 K
CorelCHART!:	●			C:\CORELDRW\CHART\	7352 K
CorelSHOW!:	●			C:\CORELDRW\SHOW\	3376 K
CorelPHOTO-PAINT!:		●		C:\CORELDRW\PHOTOPNT\	1024 K
CorelTRACE!:	●			C:\CORELDRW\DRAW\	250 K
CorelMOSAIC!:	●			C:\CORELDRW\DRAW\	982 K
Autographix Slide Service:	●			C:\CORELDRW\AGRAPHIX\	478 K
Fonts & Symbols:		●		C:\CORELDRW\FONTS\	1396 K
Root Directory:				C:\CORELDRW	1586 K

CorelDRAW! 3.0 Setup

COREL*DRAW!* 3.0

Choose which files to install

All: Some: None:

Drive: C:
Space Required: 23182 K
Space Available: 32470 K

| Continue | Exit | Back | Help |

There are several options available from the Custom Installation dialog box. You can select one or more applications and also select type and symbols to be installed. In addition, you can choose to install particular files associated with an application. For example, you can install all the files needed to run CorelDRAW, but not install the help files, sample files, or filters which let you share files with other applications.

3. To install all the files for a particular application, click on the All button next to the application name. To exclude the application from the custom installation, click on the None button next to the application name. To install only some of the files associated with the CorelDRAW application, click on the Some button.

When you click on Some, an Installation Options dialog box appears for the group of files associated with that application. In this dialog box, you'll notice that all the check boxes are checked.

4. Click on any of the check boxes to remove the check, and that group of files will not be installed.

Quick & Easy

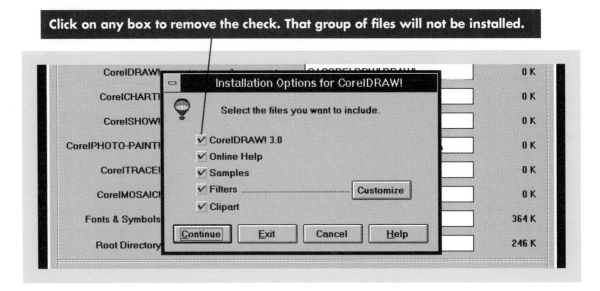

Click on any box to remove the check. That group of files will not be installed.

You do not need to install Online Help, Samples, or Clipart in order to run CorelDRAW.

5. In order to install some of the filters, click on the Customize button next to Filters.

The Filter Selection Window is displayed. All the Export and Import Filters are currently shown in the Install list boxes on the right. *Import filters* let you open files created with other applications and saved in another format. *Export filters* let you save files in a different format so you can open them in another application, or give them to someone else to use in an application other than CorelDRAW.

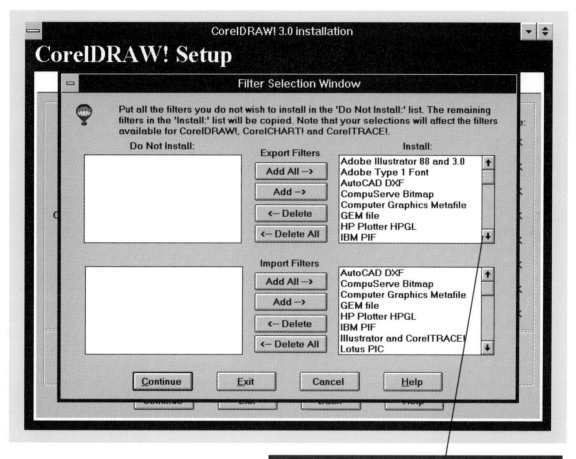

Click here to see the additional export filters.

6. To install no export filters, click on Delete All. To install only some export filters, click on the name of the filter in the box at the right, then click the Delete button. Repeat until only the filters you want to install are in the box on the right. Then do the same for the Import filters.

7. When you have finished selecting filters, click Continue.

CorelDRAW again calculates disk space and when it is finished checking, the Custom Install dialog box is displayed again.

8. Repeat steps 3 through 7 for each application shown and for Fonts & Symbols.

9. When you have selected and deselected the files you want to install, click Continue.

You'll see the CorelDRAW Setup Disk 1 progress box. The information in this box changes as the installation proceeds. If you need to stop the installation process at any time, simply click the Cancel button.

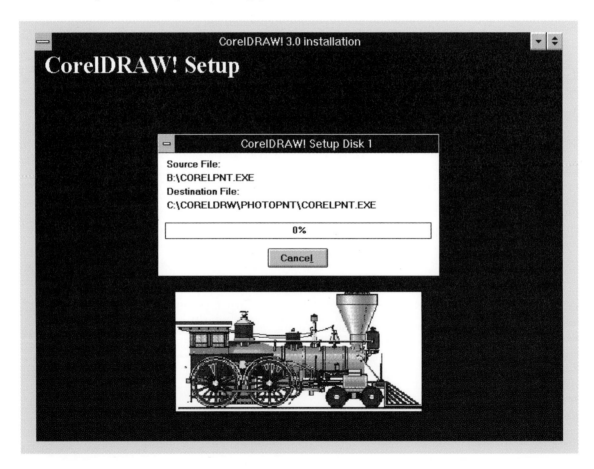

When all the files from Setup Disk 1 have been copied, you'll see the message "Please insert the diskette labeled CorelDRAW Setup disk 2 in A:" (or B: if you began the installation from B:).

● Note Since you are not installing all the files, CorelDRAW may skip Disk 2 and ask for another disk.

10. Remove Setup Disk 1 and insert the required Setup disk, then click OK.

11. Continue inserting the next disk in order each time you see the message requesting another disk.

When you have inserted the last Setup disk, go on to the next section, "When Installation is Complete."

When Installation is Complete

When the installation is complete, you'll see the Corel Graphics group window, with the program icons that let you start the Corel applications.

The icons you'll see in this window depend on the applications you installed. To start any application, point to it with the mouse and double-click.

Quick Easy

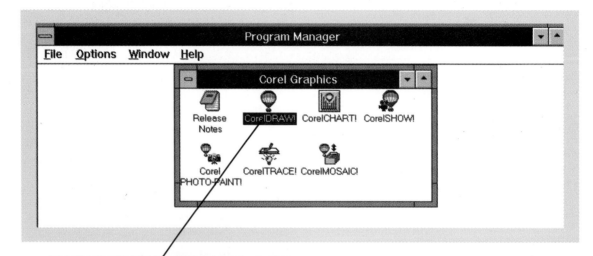

Double-click here to start CorelDRAW.

20 MINUTES

2 Getting Started with CorelDRAW

In this lesson, you'll get started creating and modifying objects and text, and begin to use the tools that are readily available in the CorelDRAW window. When you've created your first drawing, you'll also save it and print it.

Launching CorelDRAW

The Corel Graphics group window contains the program icons that let you start the Corel applications. The applications you'll see in this window depend on the applications you have installed.

1. If the Corel Graphics group window is not open, double-click the Corel Graphics icon at the bottom of the Program Manager window.

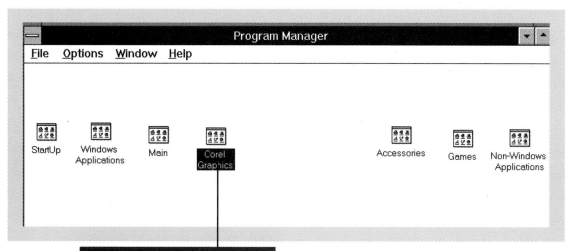

Double-click here to open the Corel Graphics group window.

Quick & Easy

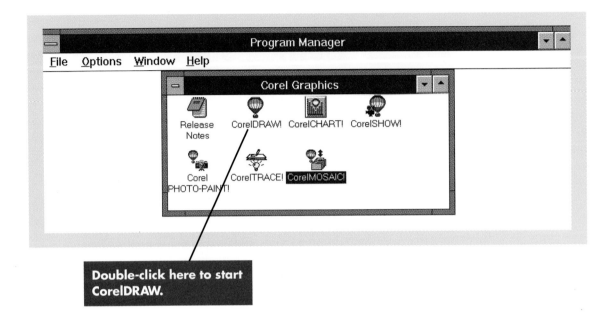

**Double-click here to start
CorelDRAW.**

2. To start CorelDRAW, double-click the CorelDRAW icon in
the Corel Graphics group window.

You'll see the CorelDRAW Application window.

The Application Window

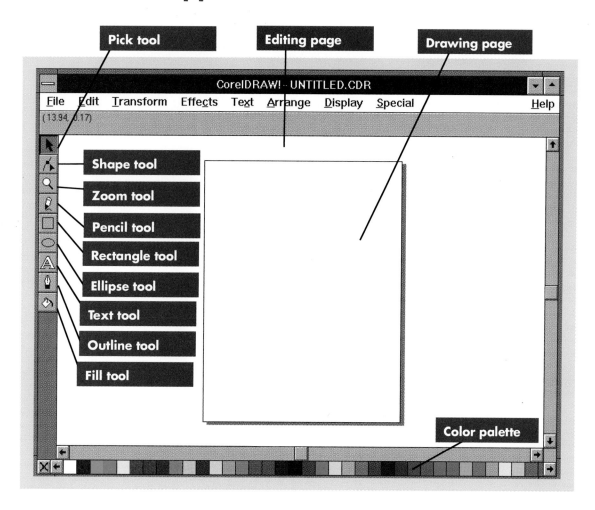

The Application window contains tools on the left that let you create and modify shapes, text, your workspace, and more. Many additional capabilities can be accessed from the menus. You have an empty drawing page on which to work. And, you can begin to work with color by selecting a color from the palette shown at the bottom of the window.

The best way to become familiar with everything is to begin drawing. In this lesson, you'll create a simple design that can be used for a brochure, opening slide, or report cover. You'll be using shapes, lines, text, and color.

Before you begin, you might want to skip ahead to the end of the lesson to see the drawing that you'll be creating during the next few minutes.

Creating, Selecting, and Modifying Rectangles

1. Click the Rectangle tool. The mouse cursor is displayed as crosshairs.

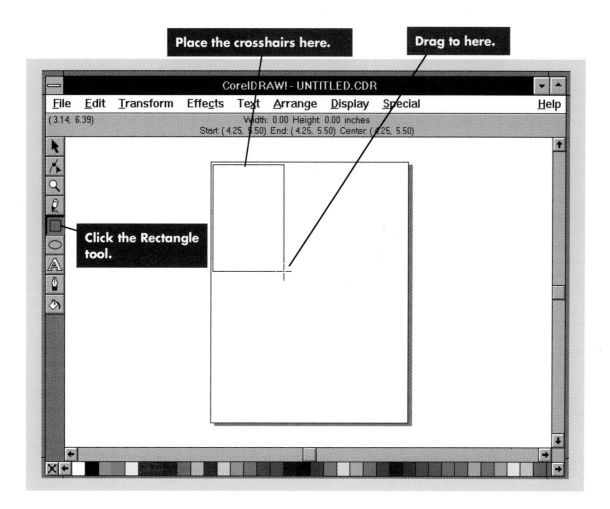

Place the crosshairs here.

Drag to here.

CorelDRAW! - UNTITLED.CDR

File   Edit   Transform   Effects   Text   Arrange   Display   Special   Help

(3.14, 6.39)   Width: 0.00 Height 0.00 inches
                        Start: (4.25, 5.50) End: (4.25, 5.50) Center: (4.25, 5.50)

Click the Rectangle tool.

2. Position the crosshair in the upper-left corner of the page, press the left mouse button, and drag the rectangle to the bottom center of the drawing page. Release the mouse button when you have the rectangle at the size you want.

You'll notice you've created a rectangle on the left half of the page.

3. Click the Pick tool at the top of the Tool Box to select the rectangle.

The Pick tool has been selected and the mouse pointer changes to an arrow. You can tell that the rectangle is selected because it is surrounded by a highlighting box, which has eight *sizing handles*.

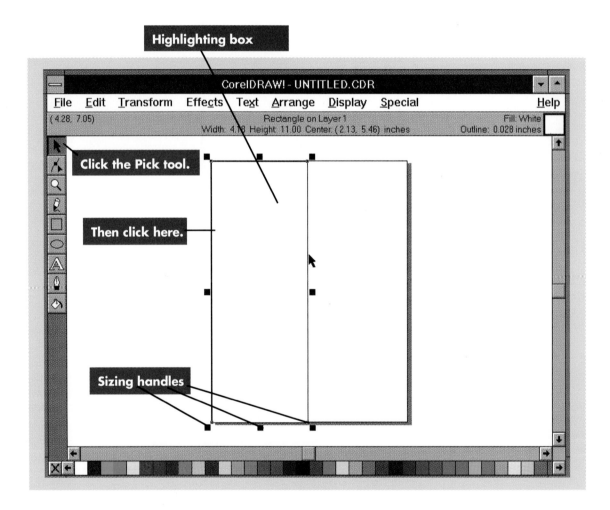

4. Now that the rectangle is selected, pull down the Edit menu and choose Duplicate.

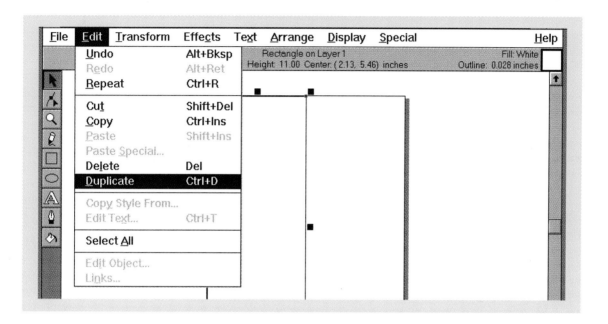

A second rectangle is pasted on the page, slightly to the right and up from the first.

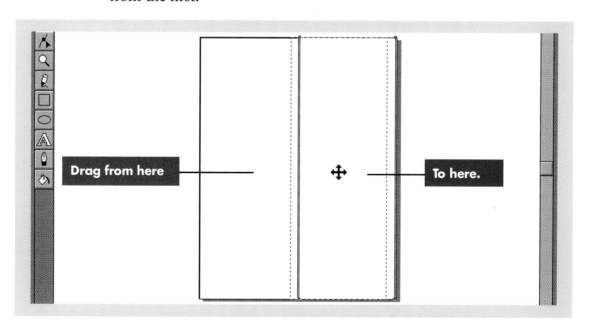

5. Position the mouse pointer within the new rectangle, hold
the left mouse button, and drag the second rectangle to the
right half of the page.

You now have a page filled with two rectangles. The second rectangle is
still selected.

6. Move the mouse pointer to the color palette at the bottom
of the screen and click a color of your choice. (The mouse
pointer changes to a black, two-headed arrow when you
move it.)

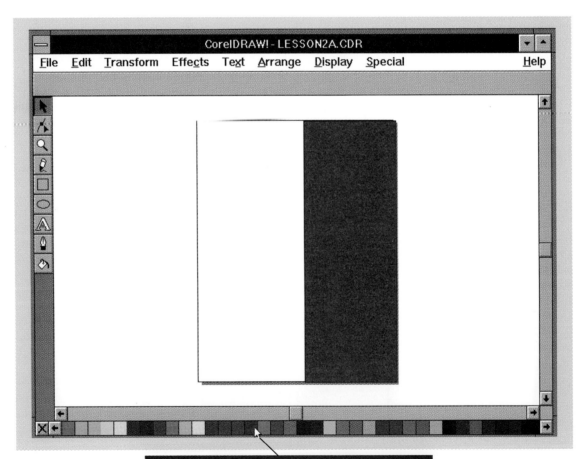

**Click in the color palette to fill the rectangle
with a color.**

For our example, we'll choose a shade of pink. You'll notice that the Pick tool is still selected, so you can select the other rectangle with it.

7. Click the left rectangle to select it.

8. Move the mouse pointer back to the color palette at the bottom of the screen and click a color of your choice. For our example, we'll choose black.

9. If you aren't happy with your selection, pull down the Edit menu and choose Undo. Then click another color.

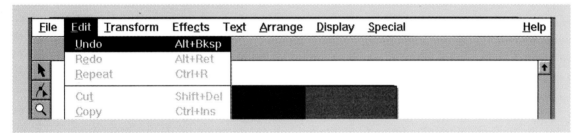

Undo always reverses your last action. Use it any time you need to do something differently as you progress through the lessons.

Drawing Circles and Pie Wedges

Now let's make some circles and see how easily they can be modified.

1. Point to the Ellipse tool and click the left mouse button. The mouse cursor changes to crosshairs again.

2. Hold down **Ctrl**, then position the cursor near the center of the page, press the left mouse button, and drag the ellipse until you make a circle about the size you see in the illustration below. When you are satisfied with its size, release **Ctrl** and the mouse button.

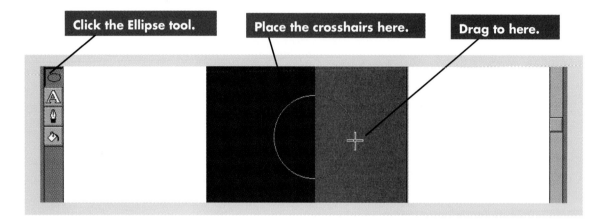

Click the Ellipse tool.

Place the crosshairs here.

Drag to here.

Holding down **Ctrl** while you drag causes CorelDRAW to create a circle instead of an ellipse.

● Note Holding down **Ctrl** while you use the Rectangle tool causes CorelDRAW to create a square instead of a rectangle.

3. Click the Pick tool at the top of the Tool Box to select the circle.

The Pick tool is selected and the mouse pointer changes to an arrow. You can tell that the circle is selected because it is surrounded by a highlighting box, with sizing handles.

4. Position the mouse pointer on the circle, hold the left mouse button, and drag the circle to the center of the page.

Now you'll turn the circle into two half circles so that you can fill each with a different color. In CorelDRAW, a half-circle or part of a circle is a called a *pie wedge*.

5. Click the Shape tool right below the Pick tool.

6. Now click the outline of the circle.

A *node* appears at the top or bottom of the circle. Nodes are points on lines, curves, objects, and text that give you additional control over modifications.

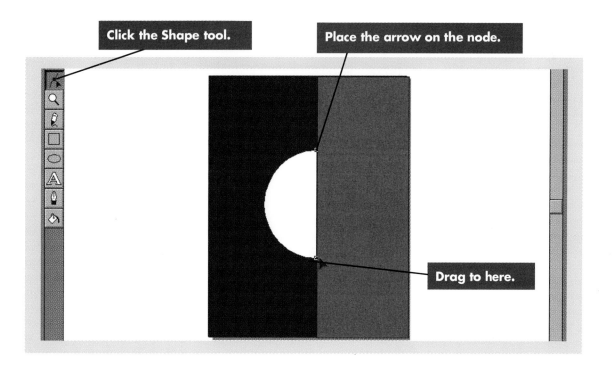

Click the Shape tool.

Place the arrow on the node.

Drag to here.

7. Drag the node around the inside of the circle until only half a circle remains, then release the mouse button.

Now to create another half circle, or pie wedge, you'll use a command on the Transform menu. But first you need to select the object to which you are going to apply the command.

8. Click the Pick tool at the top of the Toolbar to select the half circle.

9. Pull down the Transform menu and choose Stretch and Mirror.

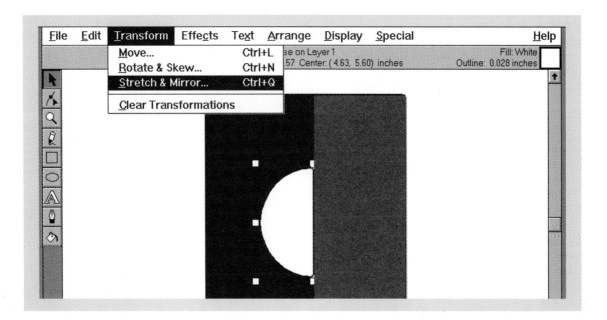

10. In the Stretch and Mirror dialog box, click Leave Original so that it is checked. Then click Horz Mirror, and then click OK.

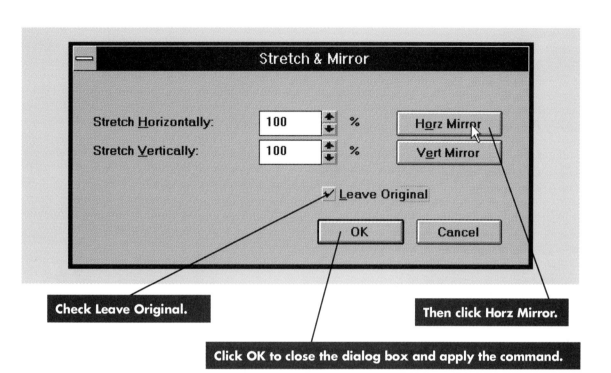

Stretch & Mirror

Stretch Horizontally: 100 %   Horz Mirror

Stretch Vertically: 100 %   Vert Mirror

☑ Leave Original

OK   Cancel

Check Leave Original.

Then click Horz Mirror.

Click OK to close the dialog box and apply the command.

When the dialog box closes, CorelDRAW creates a second, identical pie wedge next to the first, but flips it over (mirrors it). The new half circle is still selected, so you can fill it with a color.

● Note The highlighting box that surrounds the second pie wedge is still drawn around the entire original circle, but when you select a color, only the new half will be filled.

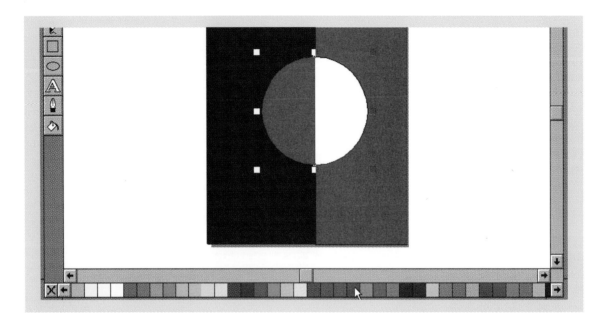

11. Move the mouse pointer back to the color palette at the bottom of the screen and click a color of your choice. We'll fill ours with black to match the opposite rectangle.

12. Now click in the left pie wedge to select it and then click a color in the color palette to fill the wedge with a color.

Saving Your Drawing

Before you go any further, let's save your drawing.

1. Pull down the File menu and choose Save.

The Save Drawing dialog box is displayed. The File Name *.cdr is highlighted.

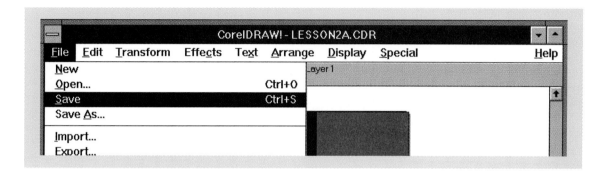

Saving Your Drawing

Before you go any further, let's save your drawing.

Click here, press Delete, then type the name of the file.

Your file will be saved in this directory.

Then click OK.

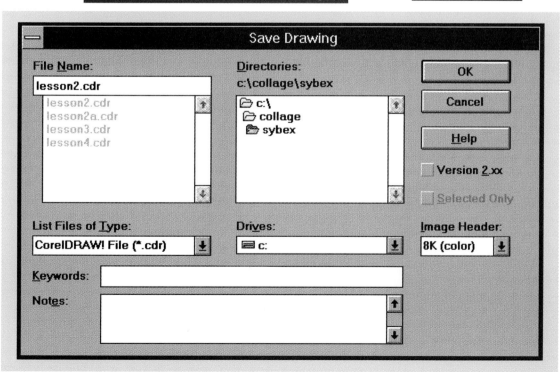

You can now type the name of the drawing. Call it **lesson2.cdr**.

3. Type **lesson2** and click OK.

The drawing is saved as **lesson2.cdr** in the directory shown under Directories.

Adding and Modifying Text

With the beginning of a background design in place, let's add some text to the page.

1. Click the Text tool. If the Artistic & Paragraph Text tool (the A) is not shown, hold the mouse button down while you point to the Symbol Text tool (the star) to open the menu, then click the A icon.

If the A is not displayed, click and hold here.

Then click here.

2. Click in the upper-left corner of the drawing page to add text to the top of the left rectangle.

3. Now type the word **GETTING**.

4. Click the Pick tool to select the text **GETTING**.

Now you can modify the text.

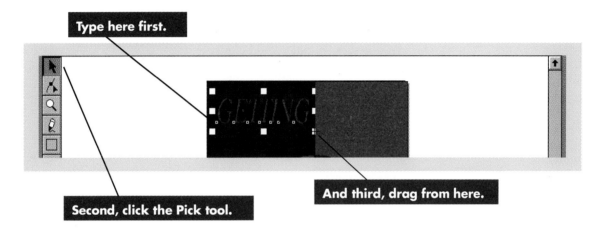

Type here first.

Second, click the Pick tool.

And third, drag from here.

5. Point to any of the sizing handles, then drag the highlighting box to make the text larger.

You can apply this technique to any of the sizing handles until the word is the size you want.

6. While the text is still selected, click a color in the color palette.

7. Click the Text tool again.

8. Click in the area next to the word **GETTING** so that you can add the word **STARTED**.

9. Then type the word **STARTED**.

10. Click the Pick tool to select the text **STARTED**.

Quick **Easy**

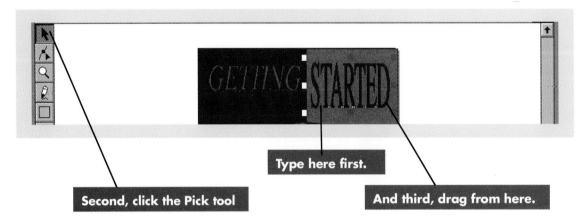

Type here first.

Second, click the Pick tool

And third, drag from here.

Now you can modify the text and you can change its size, color, font, and attributes independently from the word GETTING.

11. Point to any of the sizing handles, then hold the mouse button while you drag the highlighting box to change the size of the text.

12. While the text is still selected, click a color.

Now let's add text and then rotate it.

1. Click the Text tool again, point to the left of the circle, and type **1993**.

2. Click the Pick tool to select the text 1993.

3. Stretch the highlighting box until you are satisfied with the size.

4. Click inside the text.

You'll see eight small lines with arrows on each end. This is called a *rotating and skewing highlighting box.* You can always display this box by clicking on an already selected object.

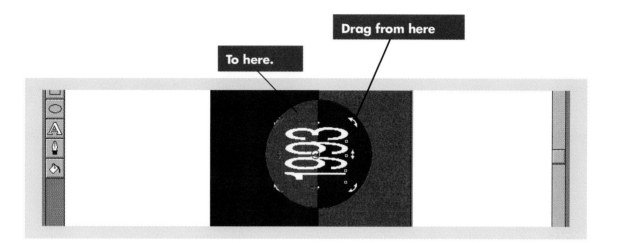

Drag from here

To here.

5. Point to one of the corner arrows until the cursor is displayed as crosshairs. Then drag the highlighting box around in a circle. When the box is rotated 270 degrees, release the mouse button.

You can rotate any object using this highlighting box. Just click a selected object to display it, and drag a corner of the box.

Changing the Outline

While you are drawing, you may notice that objects and text are outlined in a color or a thickness that you want to change. For example, if you selected the color pink for the text you just typed, you may in fact have pink type outlined in black. To change the outline, use the Outline tool.

Lets remove the outline from the text **STARTED**.

1. Click the Pick tool to select the text **STARTED**.

2. Click the Outline tool.

The Outline menu is opened. By the way, in CorelDRAW, these menus that open from the Toolbar are called *flyout* menus.

3. Now click the X.

The outline is removed.

You can apply the same technique to remove the outline from any object on the page. Just remember to use the Pick tool to select it first before you open the Outline flyout menu.

Drawing Lines

Lets add a line beneath the word **GETTING** to make the drawing more interesting.

1. Click the Freehand Pencil tool.

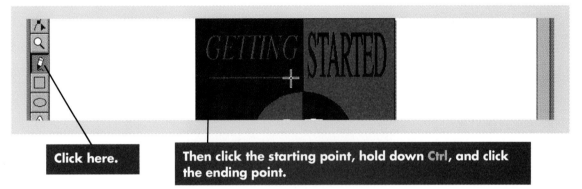

Click here.

Then click the starting point, hold down Ctrl, and click the ending point.

The cursor is displayed as crosshairs.

2. Click with the left mouse button on the starting point for the line, then press and hold down Ctrl while you click the ending point.

When you hold down Ctrl, CorelDRAW draws a straight line from the starting point you indicate to the ending point. If you want to draw a line that is not straight, for example to draw in freehand, use this tool without pressing Ctrl.

3. In fact, why don't you take a minute to experiment with the Freehand Pencil tool now? Click at the starting point, and make some lines on the page.

● Note We added wavy text to our page. You'll learn how to do this in Lesson 5.

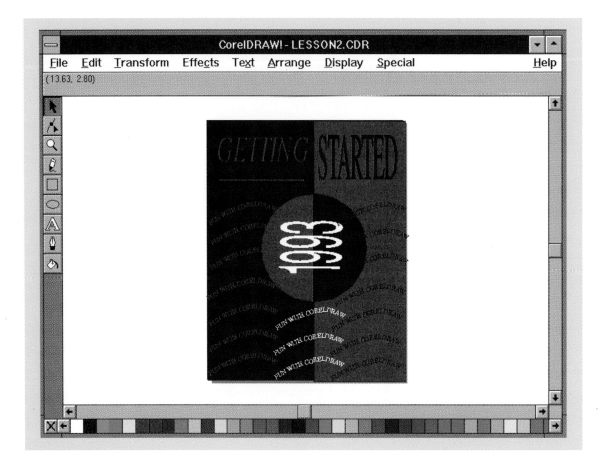

Finishing Up

Let's finish this lesson by saving, printing, and exiting.

1. Since you've changed your drawing since you last saved it, pull down the File menu and choose Save.

This time, the Save Drawing dialog box won't be displayed. CorelDRAW will simply save this drawing with the name you already gave it, **lesson2.cdr**. Now let's print it.

2. Pull down the File menu and choose Print.

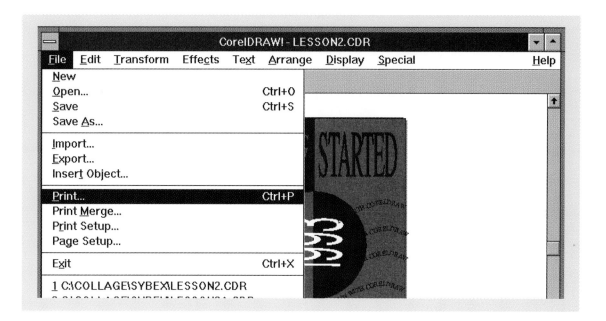

The Print Options dialog box is displayed. The dialog box and options displayed depend on whether you have installed a PostScript or non-PostScript printer under Windows.

Quick Easy

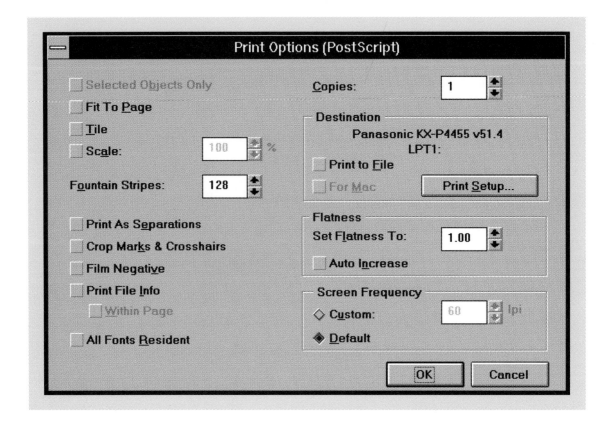

3. To print the entire drawing page, make sure none of the check boxes are checked, then click OK.

Once your drawing is printed, you are ready to exit CorelDRAW.

4. Pull down the File menu and choose Exit to close CorelDRAW and return to Windows.

1. Since you've changed your drawing since you last saved it, pull down the File menu and choose Save.

This time, the Save Drawing dialog box won't be displayed. CorelDRAW will simply save this drawing with the name you already gave it, **lesson2.cdr**. Now let's print it.

2. Pull down the File menu and choose Print.

The Print Options dialog box is displayed. The dialog box and options displayed depend on whether you have installed a PostScript or non-PostScript printer under Windows.

3. To print the entire drawing page, make sure none of the check boxes are checked, then click OK.

Once your drawing is printed, you are ready to exit CorelDRAW.

4. Pull down the File menu and choose Exit to close CorelDRAW and return to Windows.

Watch the Status Line during this lesson as you are creating and selecting objects.

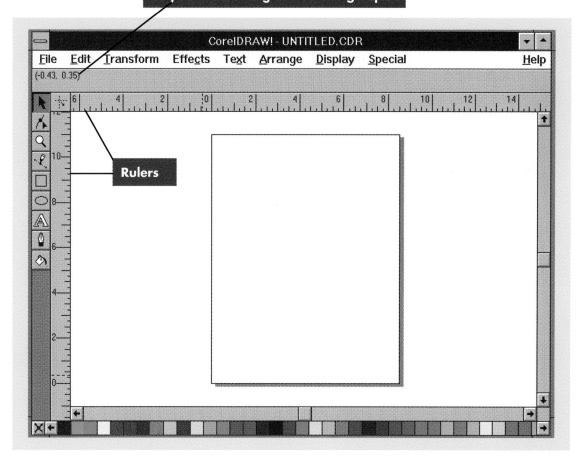

Rulers

● **Note** If either of these items is already turned on, you'll see a check next to it on the menu. If you choose a checked item, it will be turned off.

1. To display the Rulers, pull down the Display menu and
click Show Rulers.

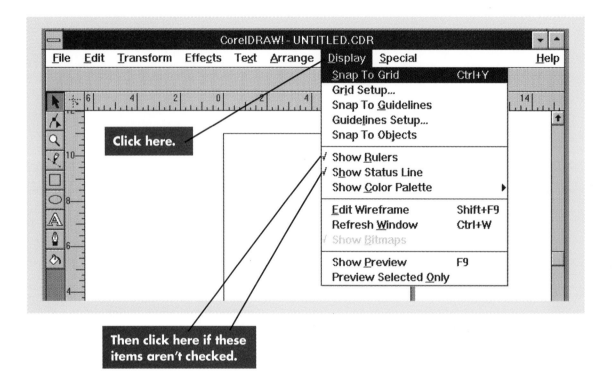

The Ruler's 0,0 point is the lower-left corner of your drawing page.

2. To display the Status Line if it is not already shown, pull
down the Display menu and click Show Status Line.

Since the page is empty, all you'll see in the Status Line right now
is the position of the mouse cursor. But as you choose tools and create, select, and modify objects, you'll see lots of information about
them in this area.

Starting a New Drawing

If you still have your previous drawing open, you'll want to save it and then start on a clean page.

1. Pull down the File menu and choose New.

Up to four of the previous files you worked on may be listed at the bottom of this menu. If you want to work on the **lesson2.cdr** file again later, click on it in this menu and CorelDRAW will open it again.

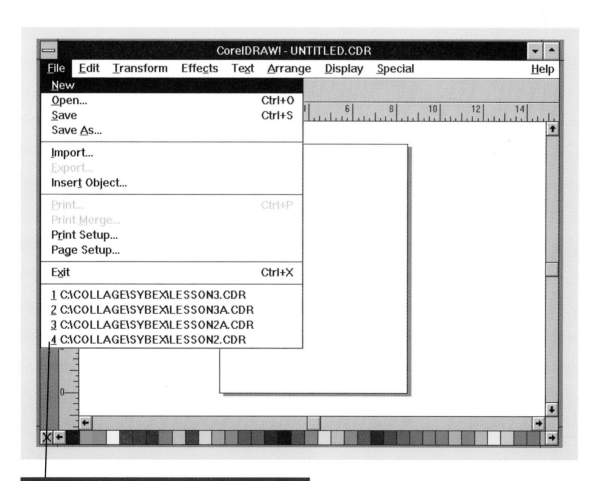

lesson2.cdr can be opened by clicking here.

2. If you haven't saved your current file, choose Yes when you are prompted.

You now have an empty page on which to draw.

Drawing with the Pencil Tool

We'll begin this drawing by creating a color background. Then we'll draw a design with the Freehand pencil instead of making a design out of shapes.

1. Point to the Rectangle tool and click the left mouse button. Then draw a rectangle that covers the entire page.

2. Click the Pick tool to select the rectangle.

3. Click a color of your choice in the color palette at the bottom of the window; we used black. If you don't like the color, keep clicking on another color until you have one you are satisfied with.

You now have a background color for your design.

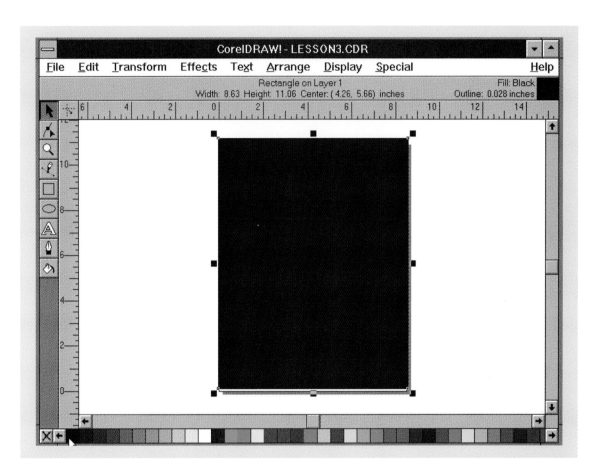

4. Point to the Freehand Pencil tool and hold the mouse button down to display the flyout menu, then click the Bezier pencil.

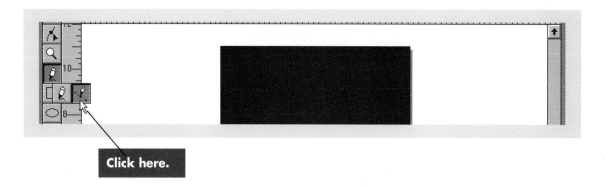

Click here.

When you're drawing, it's sometimes easier to work off to the side, until you've created exactly the object you want.

5. Now, off to the side of the drawing page, draw a leaf-like design similar to the one in the picture below. All you have to do is click the starting point and then click the ending point of each line. Make sure you make your last click at the point where you started.

Every time you click, CorelDRAW creates an end point and connects it to the previous end point.

● Note CorelDRAW has a feature called AutoJoin which automatically connects two points even if you do not draw them in exactly the same place. If you place the end point within five pixels of the starting point, CorelDRAW will recognize that you meant to connect those points and do it for you.

6. If you aren't happy, you can pull down the Edit menu and choose Delete to delete the whole object, then try again. The Bezier pencil is still active, so you just have to click the starting point and begin drawing anew.

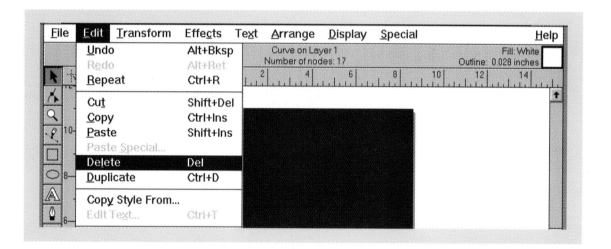

If you are satisfied with all of the object except the last line, you should instead pull down the Edit menu and choose Undo to delete only the very last line you drew.

Maximizing Your Effort

Now let's make many drawings from one drawing.

1. Click the Pick tool and then click the outline of your drawing to select it.

2. Now place the mouse cursor on a line inside the highlighting box and drag the object to the lower-left corner of your page.

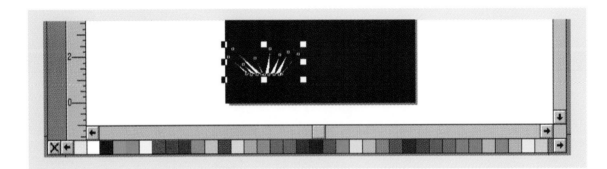

The object is still selected, so you can duplicate it.

3. Pull down the Edit menu and choose Duplicate. Then choose Duplicate again.

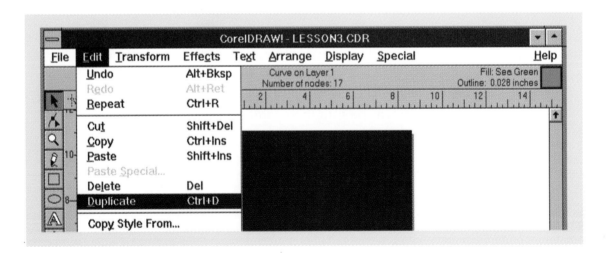

Two copies of the object are pasted on the page, slightly to the right and up from the first. The top object is selected.

4. Drag the top object to the bottom right of the page.

5. Click the remaining duplicate to select it, then drag it to the bottom center of the page.

Select all the objects to apply a command to them.

6. Hold down **Shift** while you click inside the first object on the left, then on the second, and then on the third object.

This will select all three objects, so you can apply a command to all three at the same time. You'll notice that the highlighting box surrounds all three and that the Status Line shows that three objects are selected.

7. Pull down the Transform menu and choose Stretch and Mirror.

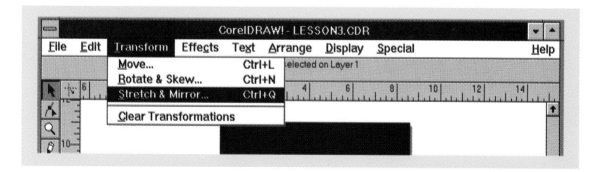

8. In the Stretch and Mirror dialog box, click Leave Original so it is checked. Then click Vertical Mirror. Then click OK.

The new objects are down at the bottom of the page and are selected.

Quick Easy

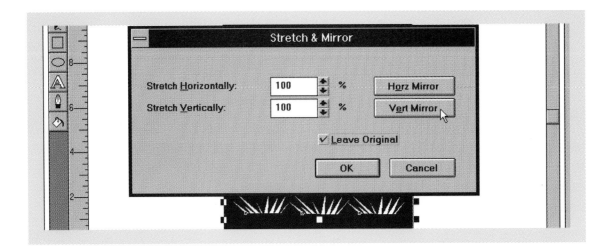

9. Click inside one of the selected objects and drag all three new objects to the top of the page.

10. Now select the three bottom objects again and duplicate them once more with the Duplicate command.

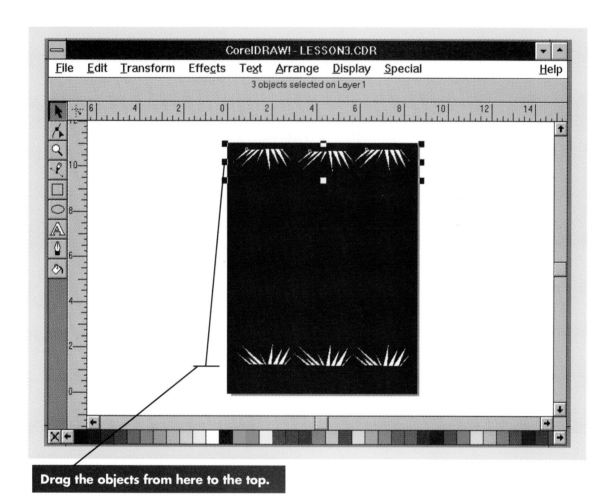

Drag the objects from here to the top.

11. With the new objects selected, point to one of the sizing handles on top, and stretch the highlighting box almost to the top of the page.

Quick&Easy

12. For a better effect, pull down the Arrange menu and choose
Back One.

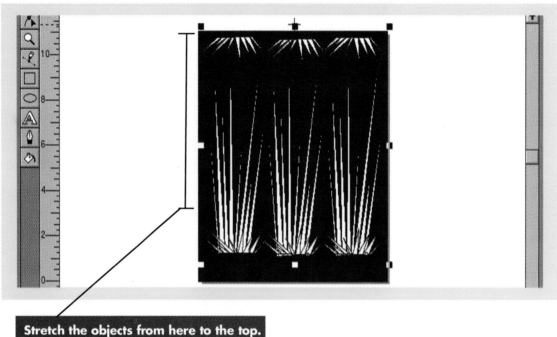

Stretch the objects from here to the top.

Choose commands on the Arrange menu, especially Back One and Forward One, when you need to rearrange objects in relation to others on
the page.

The larger objects you just created will be behind the smaller ones.

13. Now, finish off by adding color to each of the objects. Click
each one and then click a color in the color palette.

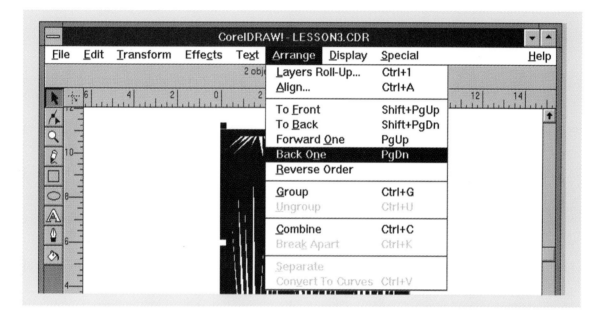

You can scroll the color palette to display more colors by holding down the mouse button on either arrow.

Rounding and Blending Rectangles

By now, you know how to draw perfect rectangles, but there are a couple of techniques to make rectangles look more interesting. First, let's round the corners and then blend two different rectangles together.

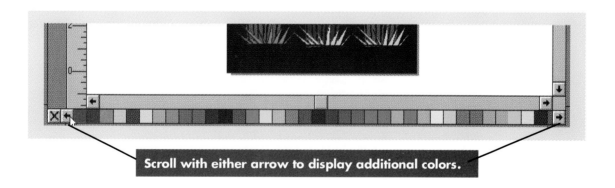

Scroll with either arrow to display additional colors.

1. Use the Rectangle tool to draw two rectangles on the page, the second above the first. Make the first 3 inches wide and $\frac{1}{4}$ inch high. Make the second $6\frac{1}{2}$ inches wide and $\frac{3}{4}$ inch high. Use the Ruler and Status Line to help you with this.

2. Use the Pick tool to select each rectangle and then give each a different color.

3. Now select the Shape tool and click the larger rectangle. Four nodes are displayed, one on each corner.

4. Point to any of the nodes and drag it in toward the center of the rectangle, but just slightly.

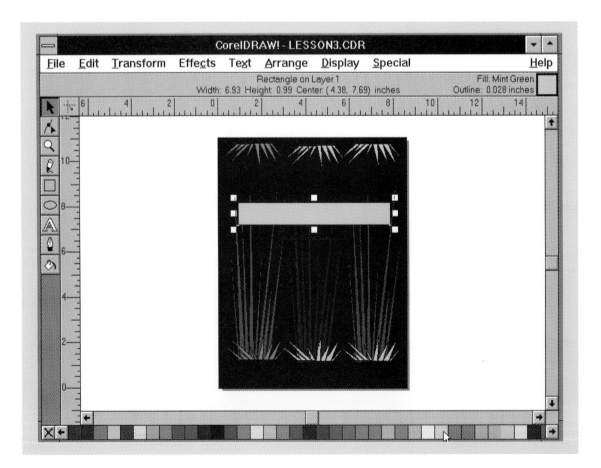

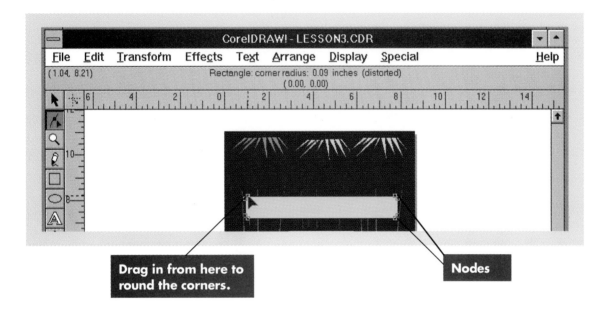

Drag in from here to round the corners.

Nodes

As you drag, the rectangle's corners are rounded. Try moving the mouse pointer in and out until you achieve the effect of slightly rounded corners.

5. Repeat the steps to round the corners of the second rectangle. Since the Shape tool is still active, you can just click the rectangle and drag a node.

Now watch what Blend will do.

6. Pull down the Effects menu and choose Blend Roll-up.

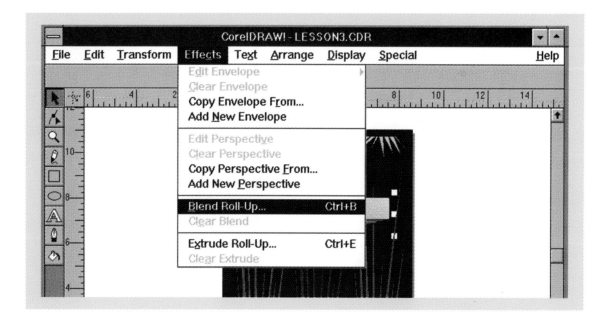

This is the first roll-up window you've used. A roll-up is similar in purpose to a dialog box, but you can move and leave it anywhere in the editing window so you can quickly access it, and "roll it up" when you don't need it so it takes up very little space.

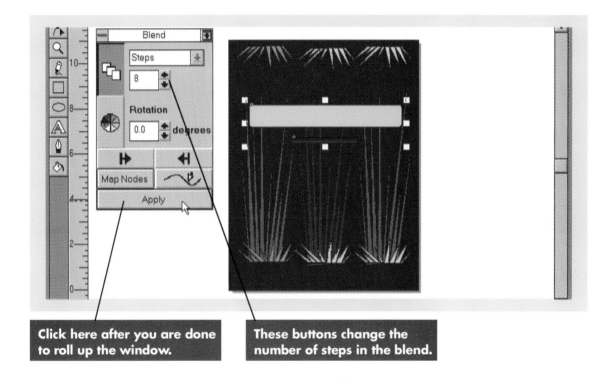

**Click here after you are done
to roll up the window.**

**These buttons change the
number of steps in the blend.**

The text box below the word Steps shows the number of steps in the
blend.

7. You can change the number by clicking on the bottom
arrow next to the number. Change the number to 8.

8. Use **Shift** with the Pick tool to select both objects.

9. Choose Apply in the Blend roll-up.

CorelDRAW blends the two objects, both the sizes and colors.

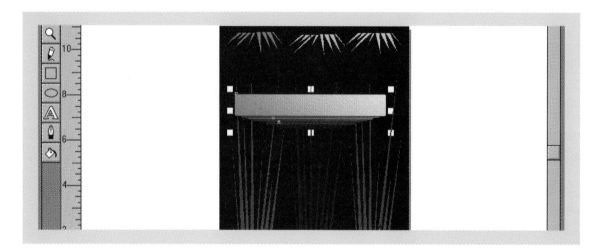

10. Click the Arrow to the right of the Blend title bar to roll up
the box. You can also drag it anywhere in the window so it is
out of your way.

Zooming In for Accuracy

Let's put one more rounded rectangle in the large rectangle and insert
some text in it. Since you are going to be working on only a small part
of the drawing for a few minutes, you may want to increase the size of
that part of the drawing temporarily, to help you work. CorelDRAW
has several tools that change your view without changing the drawing.

1. Click the Zoom tool.

The Zoom flyout menu is displayed.

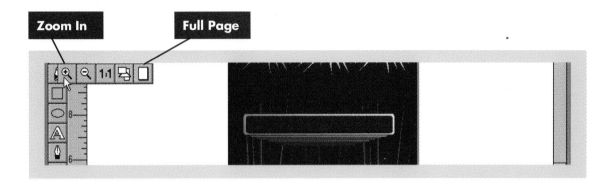

2. Now click the Zoom In tool. Zoom In is the first tool on the left, and it has a + (plus sign) in the middle.

The cursor changes to a magnifying glass. Use the cursor to draw a dotted rectangle (called a *marquee*) around the area you want to zoom in on.

3. Click at the top left of the dotted rectangle and drag the mouse to the bottom right of the box, then release the mouse button.

The area you selected is magnified.

4. Use the Rectangle and Pick tools to add another rectangle inside the large one, and fill it with a color. Look back in this lesson if you need to review the exact steps.

Now you can add some text to the rectangle and return to Full Page view.

1. Click the Text tool, then click in the rectangle to place the cursor where you want to start typing.

2. Type **GETTING RESULTS**.

3. Click the Pick tool to select the text GETTING RESULTS so you can modify it.

4. Point to any of the sizing handles, then hold the mouse button while you drag the highlighting box to make the text larger.

Stretch and drag the text to fit the rectangle.

5. With the text still selected, click a color in the color palette.

If the text is surrounded by thick black lines, you need to change the outline.

6. Click the Outline tool.

Click here to remove the outline.

7. Select a thinner outline from the flyout menu or click the X if you don't want any outline on your text.

8. To return to full-page view, click the Zoom tool, then click Full Page in the Zoom flyout. Full Page is the last tool on the right.

Adding Finishing Touches

You can put some finishing touches on the drawing that will give you additional practice with tools you used in this lesson. Let's add rectangles at the top and bottom and some additional lines. Then be sure to save your drawing.

1. Use the Rectangle tool to create two more rectangles at the top and two more near the bottom, then fill each with color from the color palette.

2. Use the Pencil tool to draw an interesting line at the bottom of the page. You can use either the Freehand or Bezier pencil for this.

3. Pull down the Edit menu and choose Duplicate to repeat the line several times for a pattern effect.

4

Creating with Clip Art and Symbols

Whether you are a professional artist or a business user who doesn't feel very artistic, you probably were drawn to CorelDRAW in part because of its enormous library of clip art and symbols. These ready-made pieces of art can help you create beautiful designs and also spruce up otherwise dull business documents when you are in a hurry. This lesson gives you the tools for importing clip art and symbols and changing them to suit your needs. You'll also learn how to use CorelMOSAIC, CorelDRAW's file manager, to find an image on file quickly.

As before, you may want to look at our final creation appearing at the end of the lesson before you start.

Creating a Background First

Before you begin putting pictures on the page, create a simple background design.

1. Click the Rectangle tool. Then draw a rectangle that covers the entire page.

2. Click the Ellipse tool. Then hold down **Ctrl** and drag the cursor to draw a circle in the bottom center of the page.

3. Click the Shape tool, then click the outline of the circle.

A node appears at the top or bottom of the circle.

4. Drag the node around the inside of the circle until only half a circle remains, then release the mouse button.

5. Click the Pick tool.

The circle is selected.

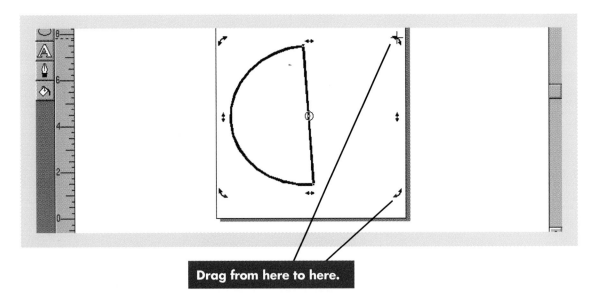

Drag from here to here.

6. Now click the circle to display the rotating and skewing highlighting box.

7. Point to one of the corner arrows until the cursor displays as crosshairs. Then drag the corner of the highlighting box around in a circle. When the box is rotated ninety degrees, release the mouse button.

8. Click the circle's outline so that it is selected and the sizing handles are displayed.

9. Click a color of your choice in the color palette at the bottom of the window. (We used a radial fill, which you'll learn to create in Lesson 6. For now, just use a solid color.)

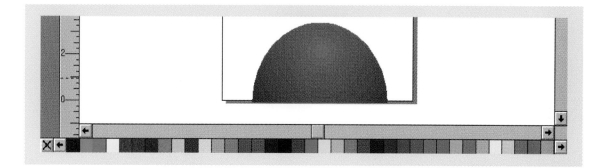

10. Drag the circle to the bottom of the page as in our sample.

11. Click the rectangle and, again, click a color in the color palette.

You now have a background for your design.

Importing Clip Art

Each piece of clip art you selected during the CorelDRAW installation is stored as a file. If you know the name of the file that you want to use, you can import the file pretty quickly.

> **● Note** The CorelDRAW package includes a manual which shows you all the clip art and symbols on the CD-ROM. The clip art that is shown in color in the manual is also included on the Setup disks, so it is available even if you don't have a CD-ROM drive. We'll use some of the clip art from the disks in this lesson.

1. Pull down the File menu and choose Import.

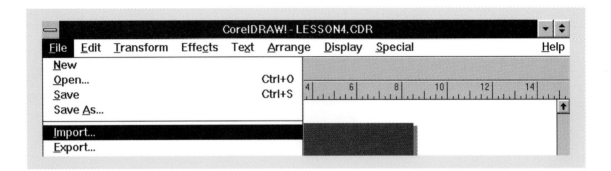

The Import dialog box is displayed. Some of the directories on the current drive are shown in the Directories list box.

2. Scroll down the list box using the scroll bar until you see the **clipart** directory, then double-click it.

3. If the File Name box does not display *.cdr, open the List Files of Type box and select CorelDRAW!,*.CDR.

4. Scroll down the list box again, this time until you see the **bird** directory, then double-click it.

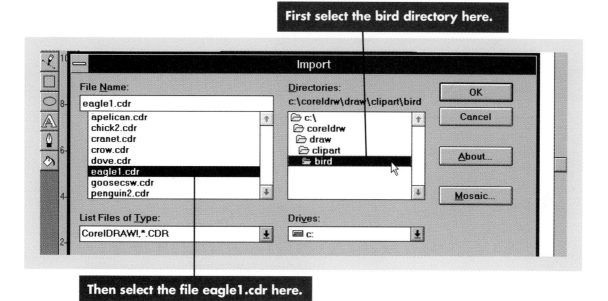

First select the bird directory here.

Then select the file eagle1.cdr here.

You'll see a list of the files in the **bird** directory in the File Names box.

5. Scroll the box until you see **eagle1.cdr**, then click it.
This is the first file you'll be importing to your drawing.

6. Click OK.

The dialog box closes and an eagle appears on your drawing page. The eagle is surrounded by a highlighting box, and it can be modified just like any object you've drawn.

Quick&Easy

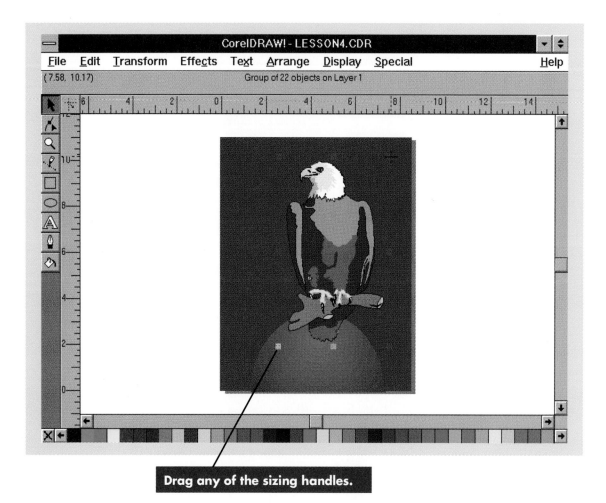

Drag any of the sizing handles.

7. Drag any of the sizing handles to change the size and proportions of the eagle, or click within the selection box and drag to move it around.

That's all there is to importing clip art if you know what you are looking for.

Viewing Thumbnails with CorelMOSAIC

If you aren't sure what you want to include but have a category in mind, you can look through a group of clip art and select what you want from a *thumbnail,* or miniature of it.

1. Pull down the File menu and choose Import.

The Import dialog box is displayed. The Directories list box still shows the directory you selected last time, **bird**. The File Name box shows the contents you displayed last time.

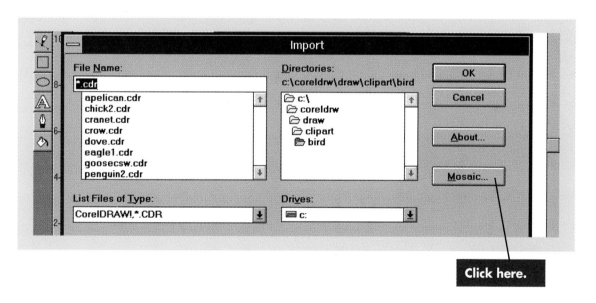

Click here.

2. Click Mosaic.

The CorelMOSAIC program is launched. The window contains the files you last viewed. If this is the first time you are using Corel-MOSAIC, no files are opened. Otherwise, the last group you looked at is displayed in the window. You can use CorelMOSAIC to show you thumbnails of all the bird files, and then import the pictures from here.

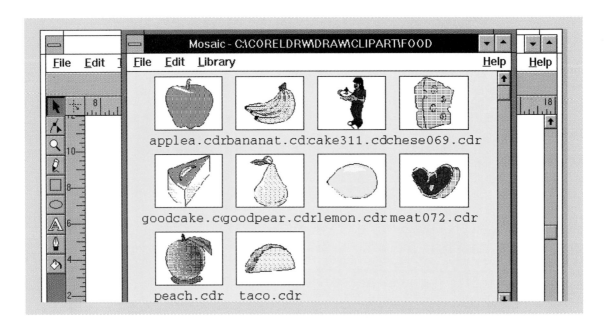

3. Pull down the File menu and choose Open Directory.

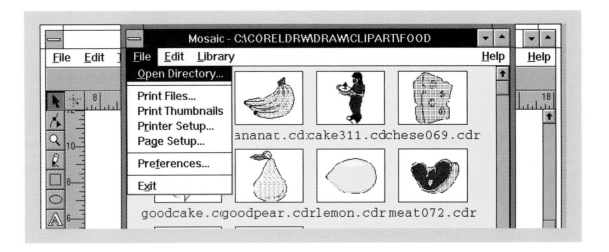

The Open Directory dialog box is displayed.

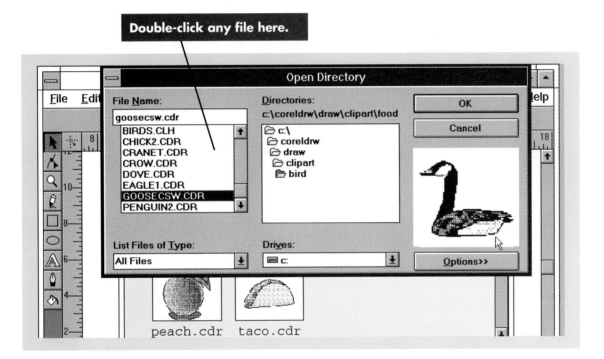

Double-click any file here.

4. Double-click **coreldrw**, then **draw**, then **clipart** in the Directories list box.

5. Double-click **bird** in the Directories list box.

6. Double-click any file in the File Names box.

The Mosaic window shows thumbnails of all the files that are in the **bird** directory.

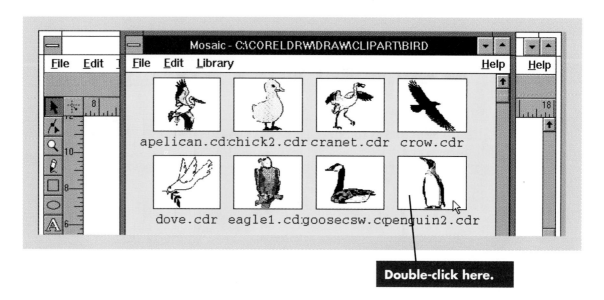

Double-click here.

7. Double-click the penguin to select it.

Drag from here to change the size of the penguin.

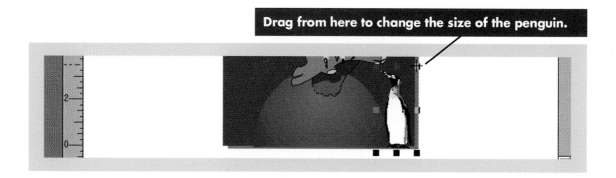

8. Drag any of the sizing handles to change the size and proportions of the penguin or drag it from within the box to move it around.

Using CorelMOSAIC Quickly

CorelMOSAIC is still running and its icon is at the bottom of your screen.

1. If your CorelDRAW window is maximized (down to the bottom of your display), click the button with the two small arrows in the upper-right corner to reduce the window's size.

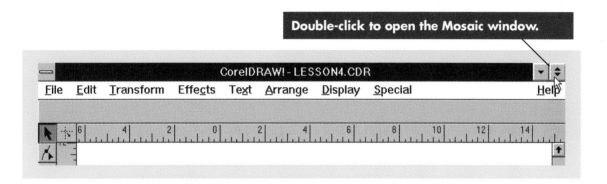

Double-click to open the Mosaic window.

You'll see the CorelMOSAIC icon below the CorelDRAW window.

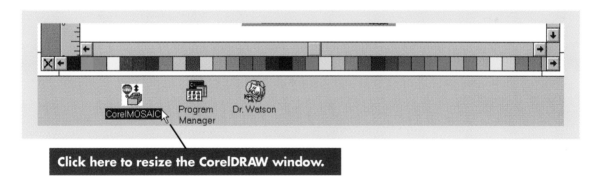

Click here to resize the CorelDRAW window.

2. Double-click the CorelMOSAIC icon.

The Mosaic window still shows thumbnails of all the files that are in the **bird** directory.

3. Double-click the crow.

You'll be back in CorelDRAW. You can resize the crow before you go on. We used four crows at the top of our drawing.

4. You can go back to the Mosaic window and click the crow three more times. Or, after you have the crow at the size you like, you can use the Duplicate command on the Edit menu three times to make three identical copies. If you've forgotten how Duplicate works, look back at Lesson 3.

• Note We also added three geese to the bottom of our drawing.

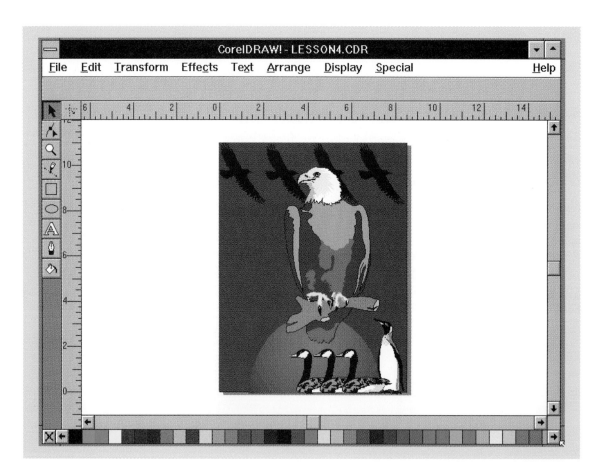

Moving Around in CorelMOSAIC

Now, let's get the other animals, which are in a different directory.

1. Double-click the CorelMOSAIC icon.

2. Pull down the File menu and choose Open Directory.

3. Double-click **clipart** in the Directories list box.

4. Double-click **mammal** in the Directories list box.

Double-click any file here.

5. Double-click any file in the File Name box.

6. The Mosaic window shows thumbnails of all the files that are in the **mammal** directory.

Quick & Easy

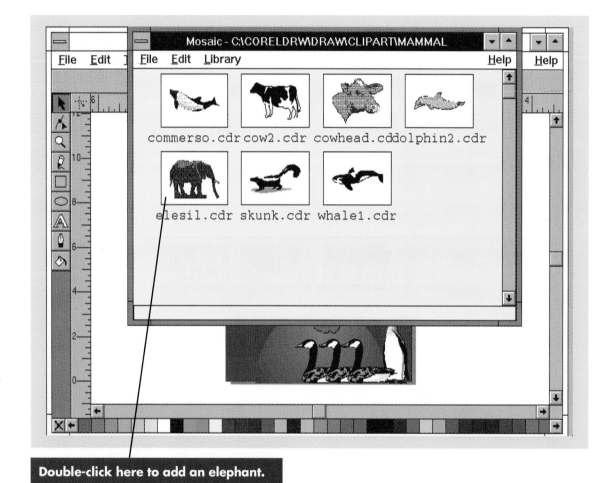

Double-click here to add an elephant.

7. Add an elephant and two whales (from the **commerso.cdr**
file) to your drawing and resize them as you did earlier.

● Note We mirrored the second commerso.

8. When you are finished, double-click the CorelMOSAIC icon, then pull down the File menu and choose Exit to close CorelMOSAIC.

If you like, you can change the color of the clip art just as you would change the color of any other object.

Adding Symbols

The other animals in the drawing are not clip art, but CorelDRAW symbols.

1. Point to the Text tool and hold down the mouse button, then click the star in the flyout menu.

Click here.

The mouse cursor is displayed as crosshairs.

2. Point anywhere in the editing window and click.

● Note If the mouse cursor changes to an arrow, the cursor is outside the editing window.

The Symbols dialog box is displayed. The list box on the right shows a listing of the symbols you installed, by category. The first category is Animals, and it is highlighted.

Click here to display more symbols.

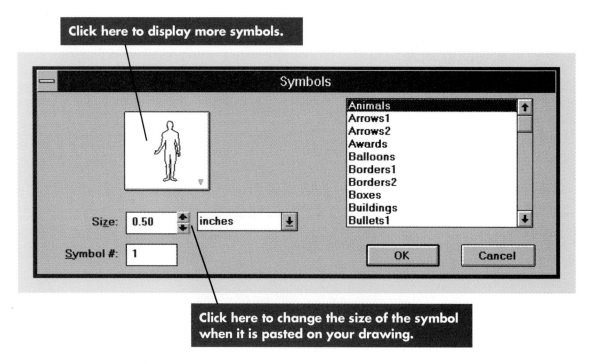

Click here to change the size of the symbol when it is pasted on your drawing.

3. Click anywhere on the thumbnail box to display all the symbols in this category.

Click anywhere in here   **To open this box.**

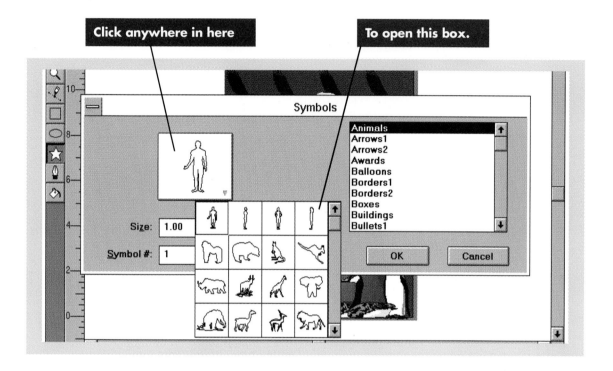

4. Scroll through the group of pictures until you find one you like, then click it. We started with the crab.

5. Change the size of the symbol to 1.00 inches by scrolling the text box.

6. Click OK.

The symbol is on the workspace where you originally clicked.

7. While the Symbol tool is still active, click again in the workspace to open the Symbols dialog box and select another symbol, and repeat the process until you have several different symbols. We added a duck and a fish to ours.

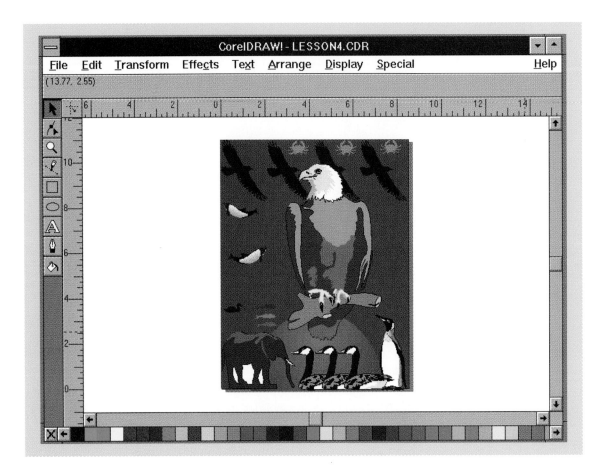

8. Now size the symbols, change their outlines, and add color, treating each as an object.

Adding Finishing Touches

We finished our drawing by duplicating the fish and crab symbols and moving them around, and by adding a seal symbol between the duck and the fish. We also added and rotated text, drew some rectangles under the text, and added lines between the text.

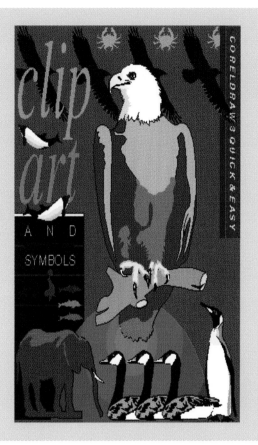

Try out some ideas of your own. Then be sure to save your drawing.

1. Pull down the Edit menu and choose Duplicate to reproduce the crab and fish symbols.

2. Use the Rectangle tool to create rectangles at the top right and bottom left, and fill them with color.

3. Use the Text tool to add text, then stretch the highlighting box to enlarge the text.

4. Use the Pencil tool to draw lines between the text.

5. Use Back One and Forward One on the Arrange menu to re-arrange objects.

6. Pull down the File menu and choose Save, type **lesson4.cdr** in the text box, and click OK.

5

Working with Text

Although you've included text in your drawings in the last three lessons, you haven't had a chance to modify the text, other than to change its size. In this lesson, we'll show you how to change the font and style and bring in text you wrote in another application, such as your word processing program. You'll also learn how to place the text on a curve, as we did in the drawing in Lesson 2.

Placing Text on a Curve

This lesson begins with something fun and easy—placing text on a curve. In Lesson 2, we drew a "wavy" line, typed some text, and matched the text to the line for the effect we created for the text "Fun with CorelDRAW." In this section, we'll also show you how to place the text along a circle.

1. Click the Text tool, then click anywhere on the page to place the cursor.

2. Type **You can match the text to any object you draw**.

3. Click the Ellipse tool.

4. Hold down **Ctrl**, press the left mouse button and drag the ellipse until you make a circle about the size you see in the illustration. Then release **Ctrl** and the mouse button.

5. Click the Pick tool.

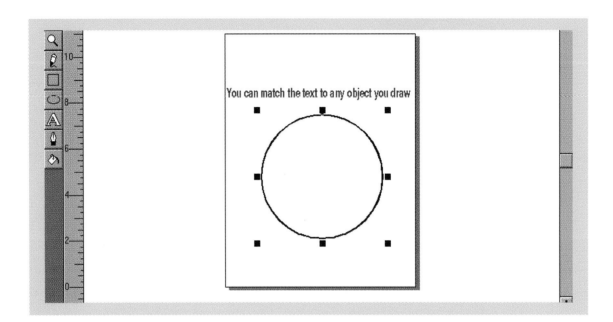

The circle is selected.

6. Press **Shift** and click the text to select it while keeping the circle selected.

Now place the text along the circle.

1. Pull down the Text menu and choose Fit Text to Path.

The Fit Text to Path roll-up window is opened.

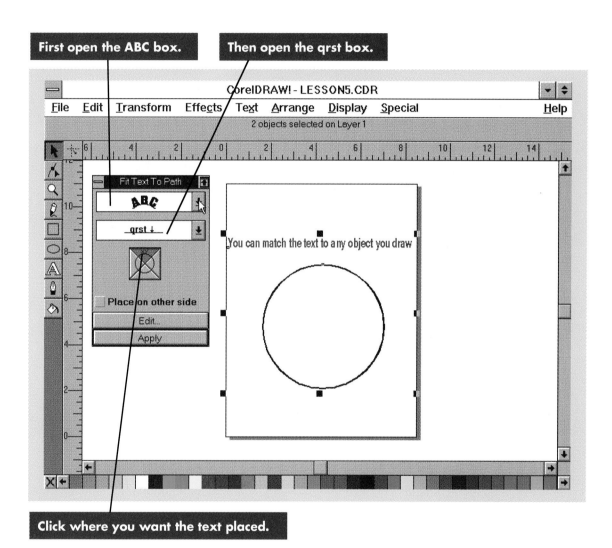

First open the ABC box.

Then open the qrst box.

Click where you want the text placed.

2. Click the down arrow next to ABC to see the different ways you can have the text curved along the outline of the circle.

3. Select the method for placing the text on the line. We selected the top row of ABC.

4. Click the down arrow next to qrst to see the different ways you can place the text above, on, or below the outline.

5. Select the placement for the text in relation to the outline. We selected the top row of qrst.

6. Select where on the circle you want the text to be placed by clicking on the divided circle in the middle of the roll-up. We clicked the bottom of the circle.

7. Click Apply.

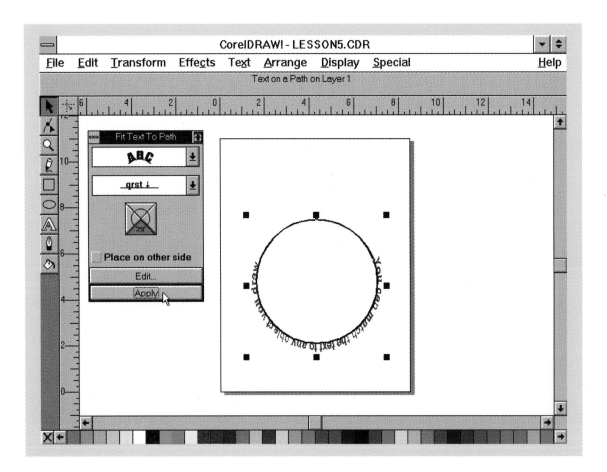

The text is matched to the circle. Unfortunately, this isn't the result we wanted, but since the objects are still selected and the roll-up is still open, it can be easily modified.

1. Change the portion of the circle where the text is to be placed by clicking on the top portion of the circle in the Fit Text to Path roll-up.

If you want to make any other changes in the roll-up, do so now.

2. Click Apply.

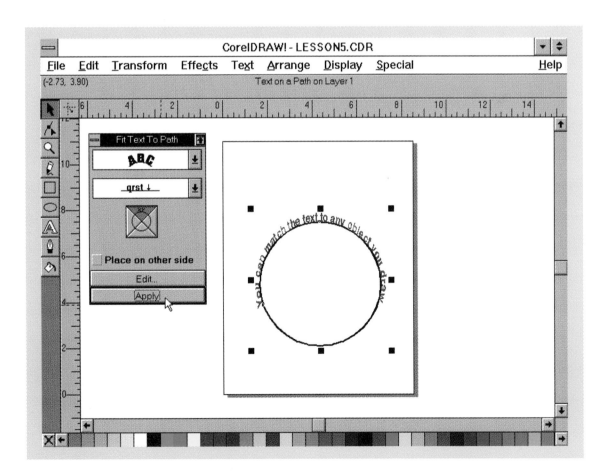

Now you'll delete the circle, since you no longer need it.

3. Click outside the page to deselect both objects, then click on the circle to select it.

4. Press **Del**.

5. Click the arrow in the upper-right corner of the roll-up window to roll it up.

6. Now, drag it out of your way.

To draw text on a wavy line as displayed in the last figure in Lesson 2:

1. Use the Text tool to place text on the page.

2. Use the Pencil tool to draw a wavy line.

3. Click the Pick tool, then press **Shift** and click the text to select both objects.

4. Click the arrow in the upper-right corner of the Fit Text to Path roll-up window to open it.

5. Select how you want the text placed on the line in the ABC, abc, and qrst boxes.

6. Select Apply.

7. Double-click the control-menu box to close the roll-up window.

Beginning a New Drawing

Once you are finished trying out the Fit Text to Path options, you'll need a clean drawing page for the design in this lesson.

1. Pull down the File menu and choose New.

2. Select No when asked whether you want to save your untitled drawing.

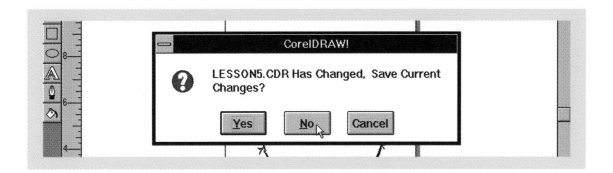

You're ready to start a new drawing.

Creating a Background

We'll create a simple background for the text before beginning. Let's first change the page orientation to Landscape.

1. Pull down the File menu and choose Page Setup.

2. Select Landscape.

Quick&Easy

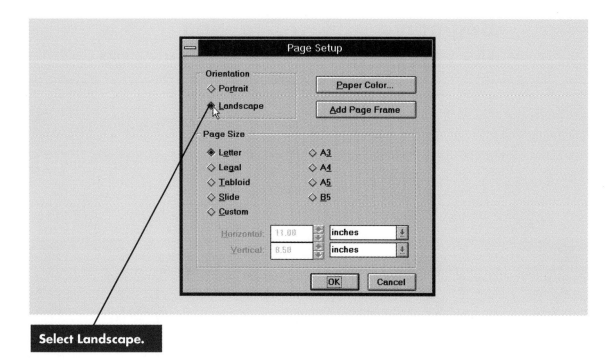

Select Landscape.

3. Select OK.

Now create a background with a symbol.

1. Point to the Text tool and hold down the mouse button, then click the Star in the flyout menu.

2. Point in the middle of the editing window and click.

The Symbols dialog box is displayed. The list box on the left shows a listing of the symbols you installed, by category.

3. Scroll through the list box until you see Plants, then click it.

4. Click anywhere in the display box to display all the symbols in this category.

5. Scroll through the group of pictures until you find the palm tree, then double-click it.

6. Click OK.

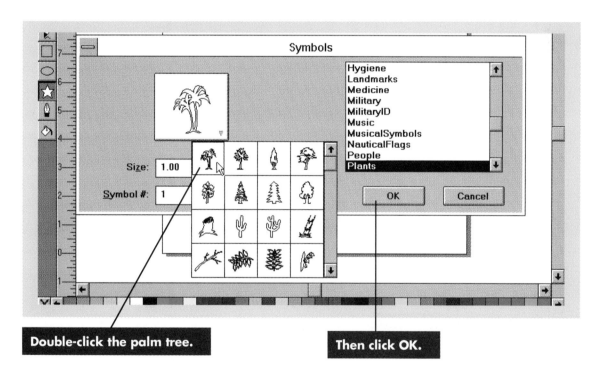

Double-click the palm tree.

Then click OK.

The palm tree appears on the drawing page where you originally clicked.

7. Click the Pick tool.

8. Drag any of the corner sizing handles out to make the palm tree larger and keep its proportions.

Quick Easy

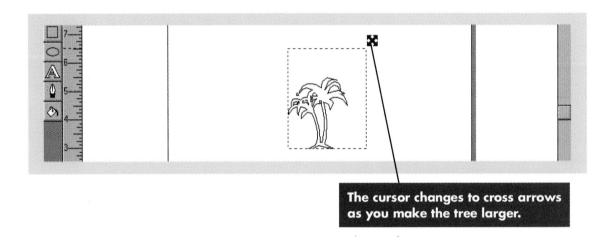

**The cursor changes to cross arrows
as you make the tree larger.**

9. Pull down the Edit menu and choose Duplicate.

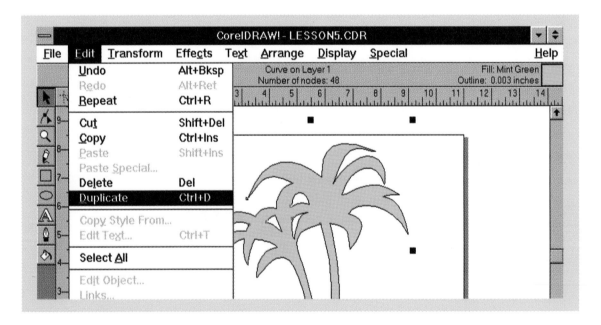

10. Move and resize the duplicate palm tree, making it smaller.

Repeat steps 9 and 10 two more times, to make your drawing match the illustration below.

You may also want to change or add color and change or remove the outline now, before you begin adding text. Remember that you can re-move the outline by clicking the X in the outline flyout menu.

Click here to remove the outline.

To complete the background, you'll add two rectangles in the upper-right corner.

1. Click the Rectangle tool, then draw a rectangle about three inches wide and one inch high in the upper-right corner.

2. Click the Pick tool to select the rectangle.

3. Pull down the Edit menu and choose Duplicate.

4. Click the new rectangle again to display the rotating and skewing box.

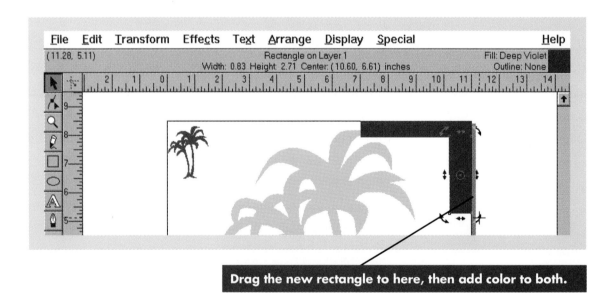

File Edit Transform Effects Text Arrange Display Special   Help
(11.28, 5.11)   Rectangle on Layer 1   Fill: Deep Violet
                  Width: 0.83 Height: 2.71 Center: (10.60, 6.61) inches   Outline: None

Drag the new rectangle to here, then add color to both.

5. Drag a corner of the box so that the new rectangle is perpendicular to the original rectangle, then drag it to the corner.

You may want to change the color and outline now, before you begin adding text. We selected the color deep violet and removed the outline.

Changing Fonts and Styles

Now you're ready to learn how to modify text. You'll type text first, then edit it.

1. Click the Text tool (Star) to open the Text flyout menu, then click the Paragraph Text tool (A).

2. Click about an inch and a half from the top of the page, near the center, to place the cursor where you want to start typing.

3. Type the following text, pressing ↵ after each line:

CorelDRAW
lets you do
almost anything
that you want
with type

Modifying Blocks of Text

To change characteristics of all the text in a selection:

1. Pull down the Edit menu and choose Edit Text.

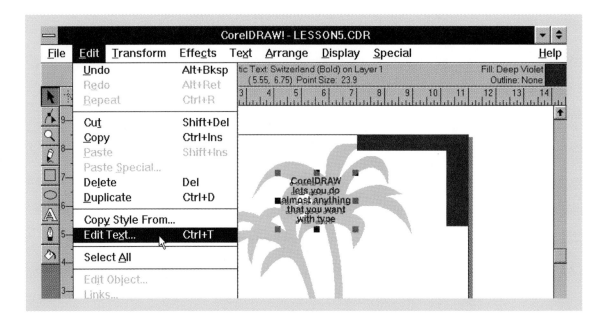

You'll see the Artistic Text dialog box. Here you can modify the text if you want to edit what you originally typed, or change the font, justification, size, or style. You can also open additional dialog boxes that let you change the spacing and bring in text from another application.

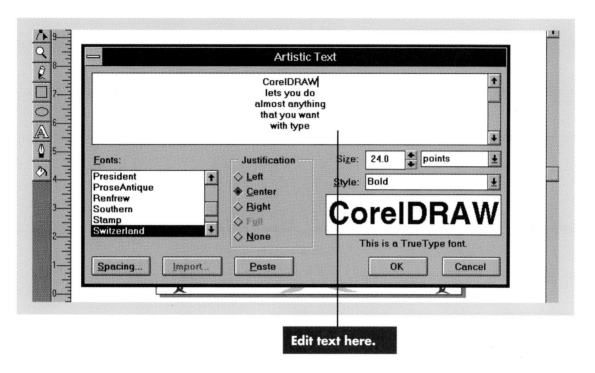

Edit text here.

First, you'll insert two additional carriage returns between each line.

2. Click in the editing box at the top, after the word
CorelDRAW and press ↵ twice.

3. Click at the end of each line and press ↵ twice.

● Note Don't add carriage returns after the last line.

Inserting extra carriage returns is a quick way of adding space between
lines.

Now that you have your text set up, you can modify it.

1. In the Fonts list box, select a font for your text.

You can scroll through and highlight each font until you find one you like. Each time you highlight a font, a sample is displayed in the box on the right. We chose Switzerland.

2. In the Justification box, select Center.

This setting causes text to be centered in its highlighting box, not on the page.

3. Change the size to 24 points.

4. Change the Style to Bold.

5. Click OK.

> **● Note** You may also need to remove the outline from the text, to achieve the result you want.

Now add some additional text on the page.

1. Click the Text tool, then click between the second and third lines to place the cursor.

2. Type **Change the color of the fill or outline, the font, rotation, style, spacing and more.**

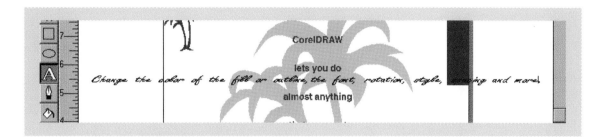

3. Pull down the Edit menu and choose Edit Text.

Now you will insert a carriage return to turn the text into two lines.

4. Click in the editing box after **outline** and press ↵.

5. Click at the beginning of the word **spacing** and press Del until it is deleted.

Once you have your text spaced the way you want it, modify its characteristics.

1. In the Fonts list box, highlight and preview fonts until you find the one you want, then select it. We chose Freeport.

2. In the Justification box, select Center.

3. Change the size to **16** points.

Now change the line spacing to increase the space between the lines.

4. Select Spacing.

The Text Spacing dialog box is opened.

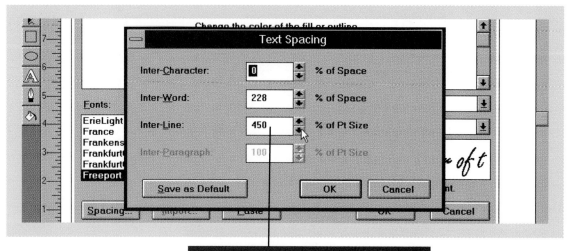

Change the Inter-Line spacing here.

5. Change the Inter-Line spacing to 450%, by deleting 100 and typing **450**.

6. Click OK in the Text Spacing dialog box.

7. Click OK in the Artistic Text box.

You should be able to add the text in the right corner, **Quick & Easy Design**, without much help. The easiest way to do this is to add the text as two separate objects, with **Design** entered as a separate object from **Quick & Easy** so that you can easily rotate it. Then modify the text attributes. We selected a different font, Penguin, for the text.

 Press **Shift** and click Quick & Easy and Design to select both text objects and modify their attributes at the same time.

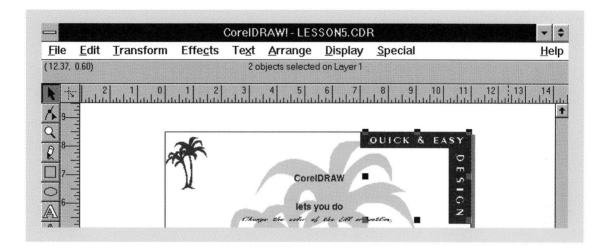

Modifying Individual Characters

Now magnify the text **Quick & Easy** so you can easily modify the individual letters **Q** and **E**.

1. Click the Zoom tool, then click the Zoom In tool on the flyout menu. Zoom In is the first tool on the left, with the + (plus) sign.

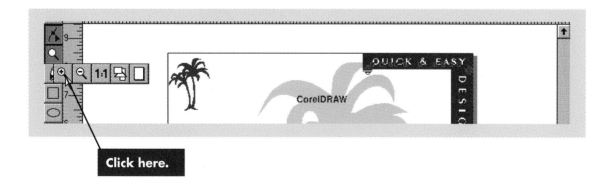

Use the magnifying glass cursor to draw a box around the text. In CorelDRAW, this box is called a *marquee*.

2. Start at the top left of the text and drag the cursor to the bottom right, then release the mouse button.

The text is magnified.

3. Click the Shape tool.

4. Click **Quick & Easy**.

You can easily see the nodes before each letter. By double-clicking on a letter's node, you can modify the letter without changing any of the other text.

Double-click here to edit this letter.

5. Double-click the node to the left of the **Q**.

The Character Attributes dialog box is displayed.

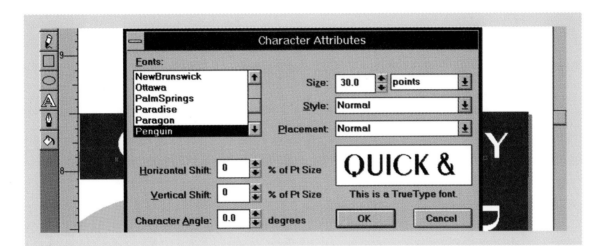

6. Change the Size to **30** points.

7. If you wish, change the Font and Style.

8. Click OK.

9. Now repeat steps 5 through 8 for the **E** in **Easy**.

10. When you are finished, click the Zoom tool, then click the Full Page tool on the flyout menu.

Importing Paragraph Text

The paragraph of text on the bottom of the page was originally created with Word for Windows and saved as Text, not in Word for Windows format. You can create text with any word processing program and save the text in ASCII format. ASCII text is text without formatting and other coding in it—it is just plain text. In most Windows word processing programs, this is accomplished with the Save As command or Export option.

To import text from another file:

1. Pull down the File menu and choose Import.

The Import dialog box is opened.

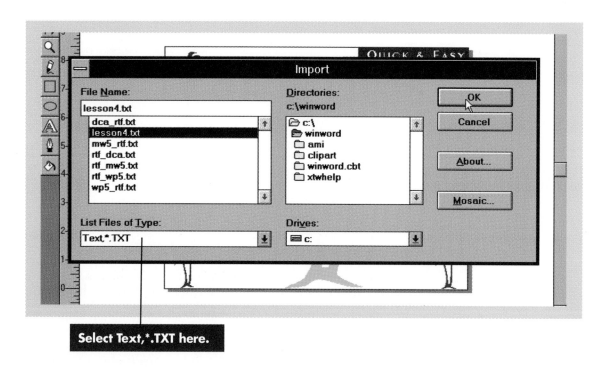

Select Text,*.TXT here.

2. Click the down arrow in the List Files of Type box, then select Text.

3. Change the path in the Directories list box, until the directory that contains the file is selected.

4. In the File Name list box, highlight the name of the file you want to bring in.

5. Click OK.

The text is placed on the page in a frame.

● Note To speed up the redisplay of the text, remove the outline from the text by clicking the X in the Outline flyout menu.

6. Resize the frame by dragging the sizing handles.

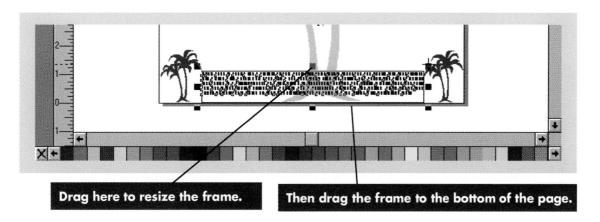

Drag here to resize the frame. **Then drag the frame to the bottom of the page.**

7. Drag the frame to the bottom of the page.

Now modify the text. You can do this in the Paragraph Text dialog box.

1. Pull down the Edit menu and choose Edit Text.

The Paragraph Text dialog box is opened.

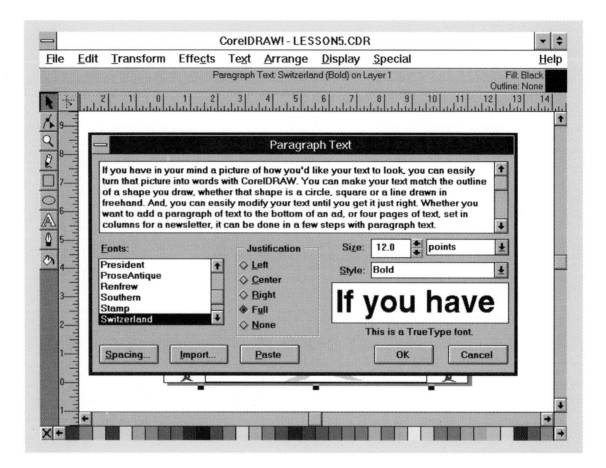

2. In the Fonts list box, select a font for your text. We chose
   Switzerland.

3. In the Justification box, select Full.

4. Change the size to 12 points.

5. Click OK.

Finishing Touches

As always, we recommend you save and print your hard work. You may also want to try achieving some different effects with text before you go on to Lesson 6.

Our finished design is shown below.

Doing More with Objects

6

Until now, you've been working primarily with on-screen tools, flyout menus, and roll-up windows to create and modify objects. In this lesson, you'll have a chance to try out some additional modification techniques, like filling objects with radial fills. You'll learn how to skew and reshape objects, combine them, and align them.

Setting Up a Background

If you have just finished Lesson 5, you'll need to change the page orientation back to portrait for this lesson.

1. Pull down the File menu and choose Page Setup. The Page Setup dialog box is opened.

2. Select Portrait.

3. Click Add Page Frame.

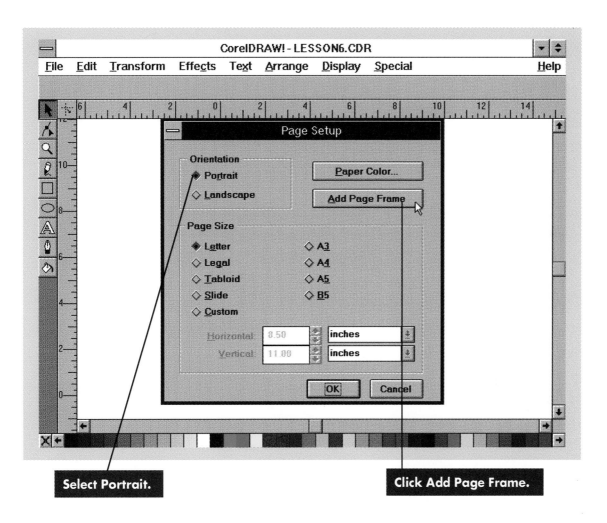

Select Portrait.

Click Add Page Frame.

Instead of drawing a rectangle on the page, you can use the Add Page Frame button to automatically draw a rectangle that matches the page size.

4. Click OK.

Selecting Fountain Fills

The page frame has no fill by default. You will provide the frame with a *fountain fill.* A fountain fill is a blend of two colors or tints of colors.

1. Click the Fill tool, then click the Fountain fill icon on the flyout menu.

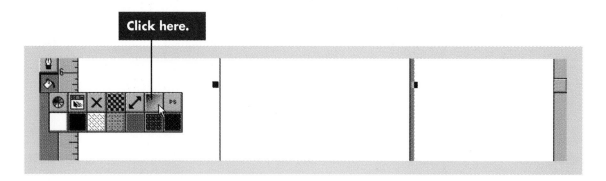

The Fountain Fill dialog box is displayed.

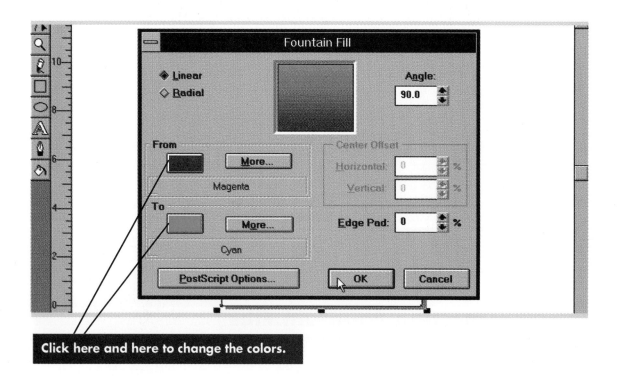

2. Click the color shown beneath From to display a color palette.

3. In the color palette, click on a color to begin the fountain fill. We chose magenta.

4. Click the color shown beneath To to display a color palette.

5. In the color palette, click on a color to end the fountain fill. We chose cyan.

6. Click OK.

The page frame now has the linear fountain fill you selected.

Fills in Solid Objects

Next, you'll add an ellipse and fill it with a radial fountain fill.

1. Click the Ellipse tool.

2. Place the cursor at the left edge, halfway down the page and drag the ellipse to the right edge, as in the illustration.

3. Click the Pick tool. The ellipse is selected.

4. Click the Fill tool, then click the Fountain fill icon on the flyout menu.

5. In the Fountain Fill dialog box, select Radial to change the color from the center outward.

6. Click the color shown beneath From to display a color palette.

7. In the color palette, click on a color. We chose Twilight Blue.

8. Click the color shown beneath To to display a color palette.

9. In the color palette, click on a color. We chose Sky Blue.

10. Click OK.

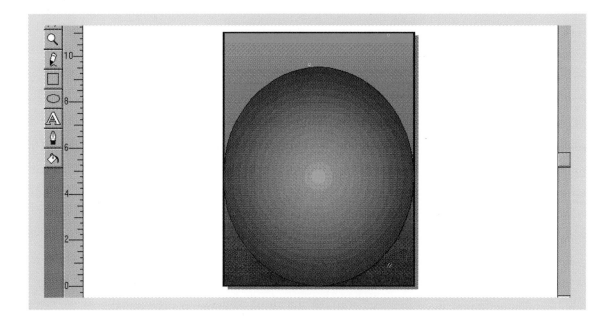

The ellipse now has the radial fountain fill you selected.

Fills in Blends

Now let's see how to blend colors when you blend shapes.

1. Use the Rectangle tool to draw two rectangles on the page, the first near the bottom of the circle (about .6" wide and .3" high) and the second near the top of the circle and larger (about 6.75" wide and 1.0" high).

2. Use the Pick tool to select each rectangle and then give each a different solid color.

We chose blue for the bottom and magenta for the top rectangle.

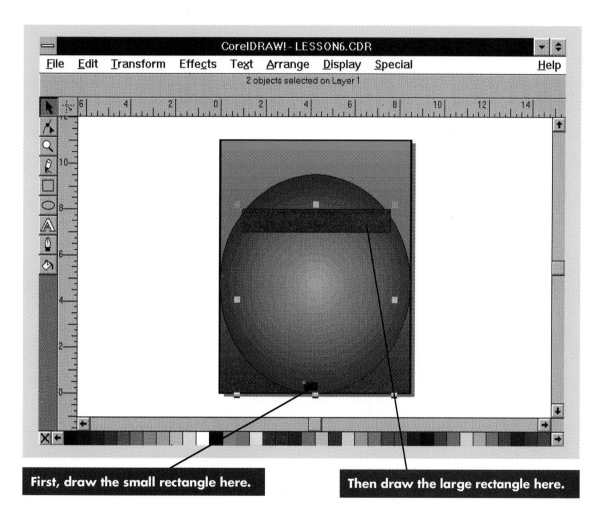

First, draw the small rectangle here.

Then draw the large rectangle here.

3. Use **Shift** with the Pick tool to select both objects.

4. Pull down the Effects menu and choose Blend Roll-up.

5. Change the number of steps to **20.**

6. Click the rainbow button.

7. Check the Rainbow check box.

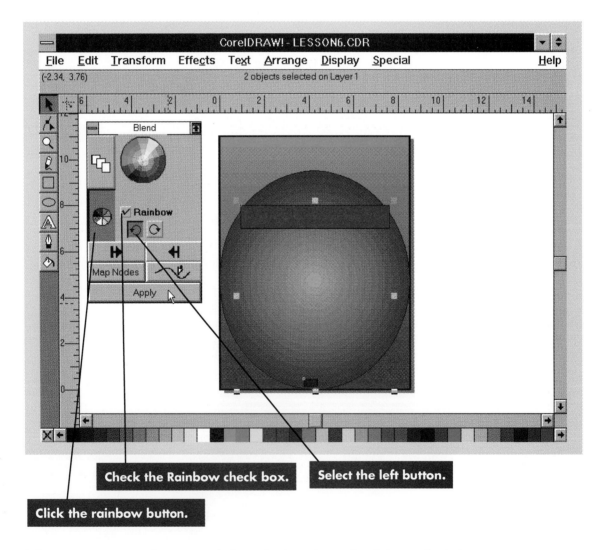

Click the rainbow button.

Check the Rainbow check box.

Select the left button.

There are two circular arrows below the Rainbow check box which let you indicate how you want the colors blended.

8. Select the left button, which shows the arrow in a counter-clockwise direction.

9. Click Apply.

Your rectangles will be blended with a rainbow of colors. If your rectangles look different than those in the illustration, you probably created the top rectangle first, instead of the bottom rectangle. This would cause CorelDRAW to blend from the top down instead of the bottom up, as in our illustration.

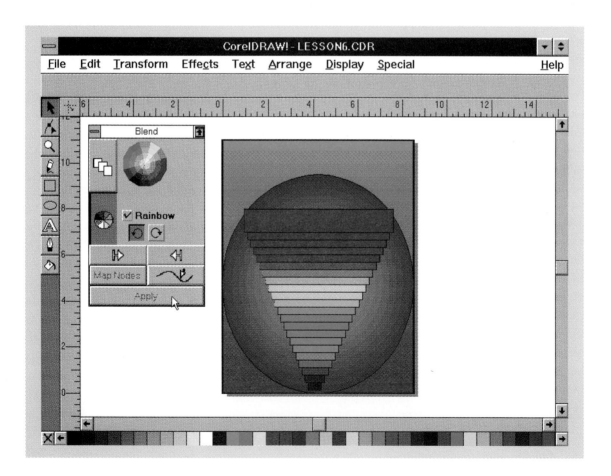

Changing Lines

Now you'll use some different tools to draw a pinwheel-shaped object to place at the top of the page behind the ellipse. It is easier to draw this to the right of the drawing page and then place it on the page when it's finished.

1. Click the Pencil tool.

2. Click on the starting point for the line, then press and hold down **Ctrl** while you click the ending point. Draw a line about six inches long.

3. Click the Outline tool.

4. In the Outline flyout menu, click the Pen.

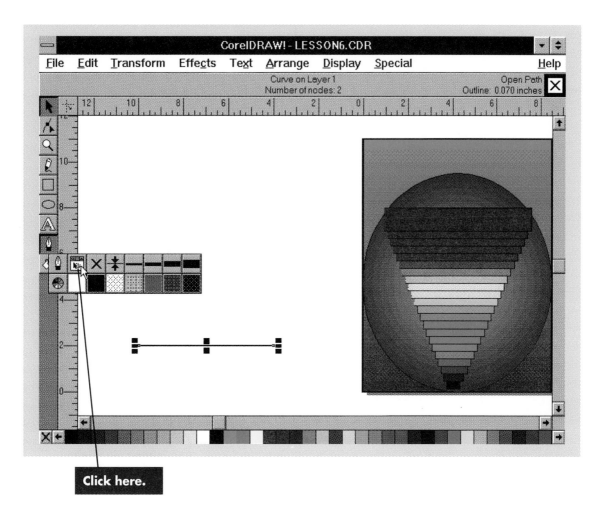

Click here.

The Pen roll-up window is opened. The top box lets you change the thickness.

Click and hold here to change the line thickness.

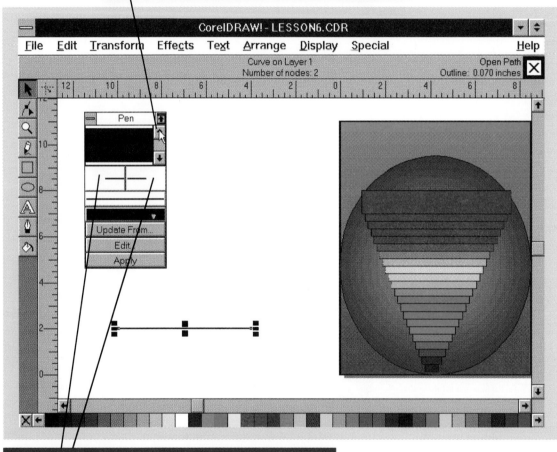

Click here or here to change the line into an arrow.

5. Click and hold the top arrow until the maximum thickness
is achieved.

6. Click on the line ending box to open a display box with
arrows and line endings.

7. Click on an arrowhead.

8. Click Apply.

Actually, we won't need an arrow for this drawing, so let's go back and change this line ending. The Pen roll-up is still open, so it's easy to modify the line, which is still selected.

1. Click on the line ending box to open the display box with arrows and line endings.

2. Click on the plain line ending which is in the upper-left corner.

3. Click Apply.

4. Roll up the Pen roll-up window by clicking the arrow in the upper-right corner.

Now change the color of the line.

1. Click the Outline tool again.

2. In the Outline flyout menu, click the first tool.

The Outline Pen dialog box is opened; you can change outline characteristics here.

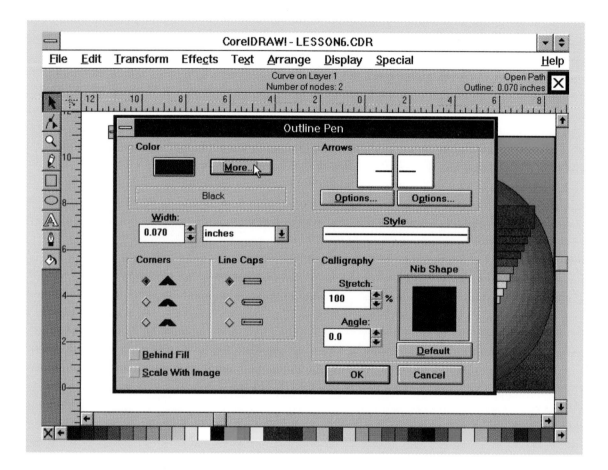

3. Click the More button near the upper-left corner of the box.

The Outline Color dialog box is displayed; you can change the
color of the outline here.

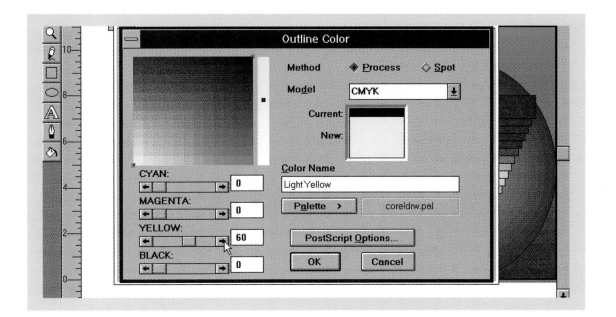

4. Use the scroll bars to change the color to **60%** Yellow and **0%** Cyan, Magenta, and Black.

5. Click OK.

The Outline Pen dialog box is displayed again.

6. In the Line Caps box, select the middle option to round the ends of the line.

7. Click OK.

You'll have a thick yellow line with rounded ends. Use this line as the basis of your pinwheel.

This line can be transformed into a pinwheel.

Repeating Transformations

You can use the Repeat command to easily duplicate and rotate the line, once you enter the Rotation Angle in the Rotate and Skew dialog box.

1. Click the Pick tool. The line is selected.

2. Pull down the Transform menu and choose Rotate and Skew. The Rotate and Skew dialog box is displayed.

3. Change the rotation angle to 20 degrees.

4. Check Leave Original.

5. Click OK. The object is duplicated and rotated.

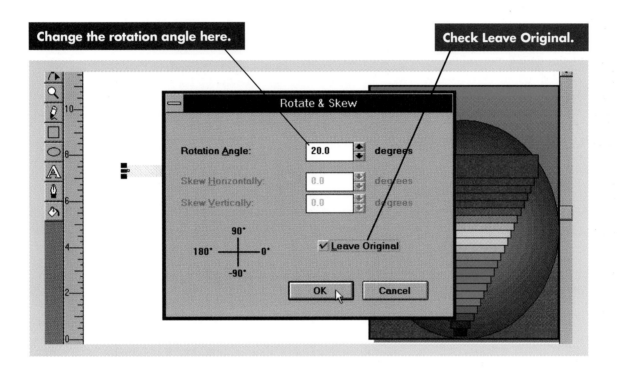

Change the rotation angle here.

Check Leave Original.

Rotate & Skew

Rotation Angle: 20.0 degrees

Skew Horizontally: 0.0 degrees

Skew Vertically: 0.0 degrees

90°

180° — 0°

-90°

☑ Leave Original

OK   Cancel

6. Pull down the Edit menu and choose Repeat.

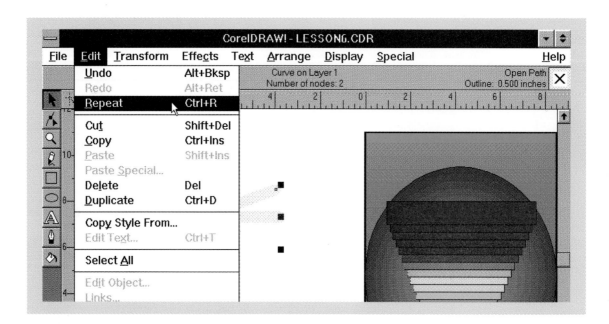

The transformation is repeated.

> **7.** Continue choosing Repeat until you've created a full rotation of lines.

Grouping and Arranging

Once the pinwheel is completed, you can move it to the drawing page.

> **1.** Draw a selection box around the group of objects by clicking at the top left of the group and dragging to the bottom right.

In CorelDRAW, this is called *marquee selecting.*

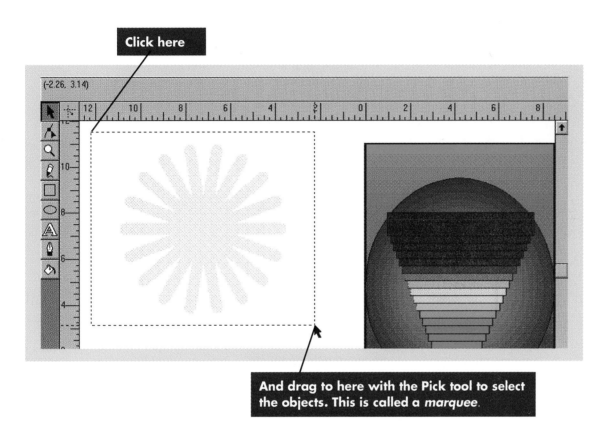

Click here

(-2.26, 3.14)

And drag to here with the Pick tool to select the objects. This is called a *marquee*.

2. Pull down the Arrange menu and choose Group.

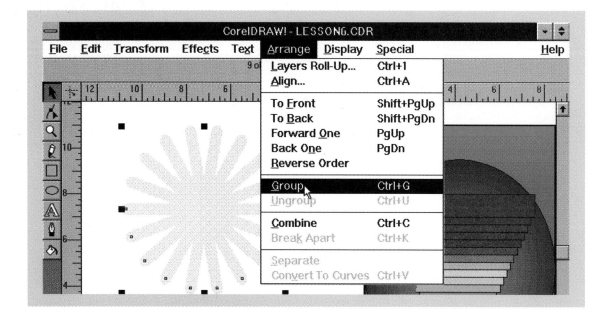

With the objects grouped, it is easier to select, modify, and position
them together.

3. Drag the group of objects almost to the top of the page.

4. Pull down the Arrange menu and choose To Back to move
the object behind the page fill.

5. Then pull down the Arrange menu and choose Forward
One to move the pinwheel so that it is behind the ellipse.

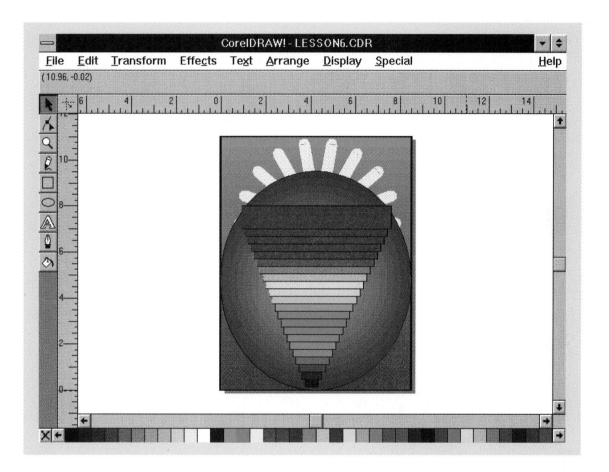

Connecting Curves and Nodes

Next, you'll create two small, half-circular objects for the upper corners of the page.

1. Click the Ellipse tool.

2. Press **Ctrl** and draw a circle about two inches in diameter off to the left of the drawing page.

3. Click the Shape tool.

4. Select the node and drag it clockwise along the outside of the circle until you have an ellipse whose total angle is 90 degrees.

Look in the Status Line as you are drawing to see how the angle changes.

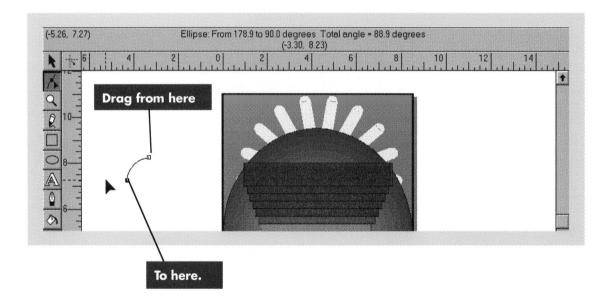

5. Click the Pick tool. The arc is selected.

6. Pull down the Arrange menu and choose Convert to Curves.

The object is displayed with two nodes, one at each end of the curve.

7. Click the Zoom tool, then click the Zoom In tool on the fly-out menu.

8. Draw a marquee around the curve with the zoom cursor.

9. Click the Freehand Pencil tool.

10. Draw a line from one end of the arc to the other by clicking one node, then clicking the other node.

The object is now a closed path.

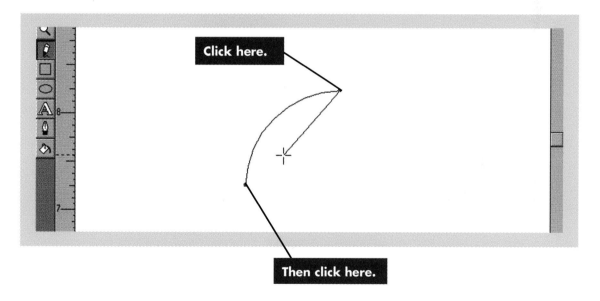

Click here.

Then click here.

Now finish it off.

1. Click the Zoom tool, then click the Full Page tool on the fly-out menu.

2. Click the Pick tool.

3. Select a color from the color palette to fill it.

4. Click on the object to display the rotating and skewing box.

5. Drag one of the sizing handles around so the flat side of the object is on the left.

6. Click on the object to display the highlighting box.

7. Drag the object to the upper-left corner of the page.

Create another object for the right corner.

1. Pull down the Transform menu and choose Rotate and Skew.

2. In the Rotate and Skew dialog box, check Leave Original.

3. Change the Rotation Angle to **180%**.

4. Click OK.

5. Drag the new object to the right corner of the page.

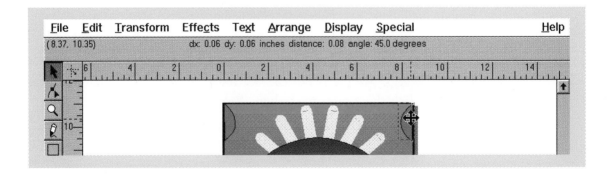

Editing Envelopes

In CorelDRAW, you can change the shape of an object, even a symbol or clip art, by editing its *envelope.* An envelope is similar to a highlighting box, but differs in that you can change its shape in many different ways.

1. Pull down the File menu and choose Import.

The Import dialog box is opened.

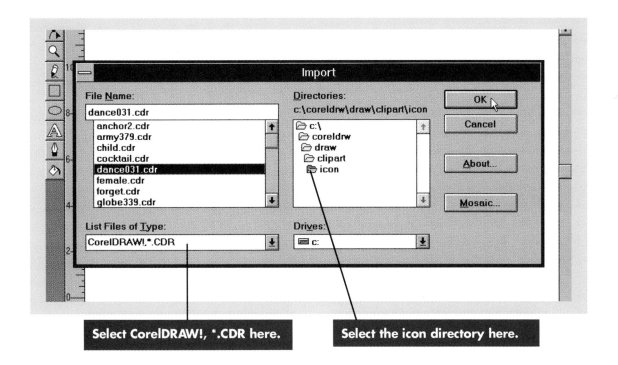

Select CorelDRAW!, *.CDR here.

Select the icon directory here.

2. Scroll down the Directories list box until you see the **coreldrw** directory, then double-click it. Then double-click **draw**.

3. In the Directories list box, double-click the **clipart** directory. Then scroll down and double-click the **icon** directory.

4. Open the List Files of Type box and select CorelDRAW!,*.CDR.

5. Scroll the File Name box until you see **dance031.cdr**, then click it.

6. Click OK.

The dialog box closes and two dancers are on your drawing page. The object is surrounded by a highlighting box.

You're going to create four additional objects like the dancers. And you'll modify them so they don't look exactly the same.

1. Drag the object to the left of the drawing page.

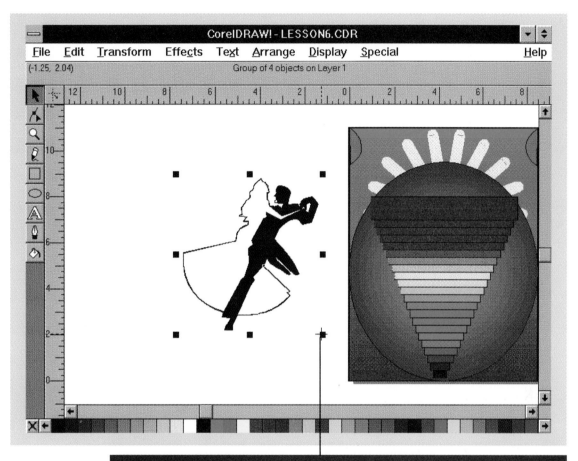

Drag from here to make the object smaller while keeping its proportions.

2. Drag a corner sizing handle in to make the object smaller and keep its proportions.

3. Pull down the Edit menu and choose Duplicate.

4. Drag the object to the side.

Now modify the new object so it looks a little different.

5. Pull down the Effects menu and choose Edit Envelope.

Another menu with four editing modes appears.

6. Click the bottom shape, which lets you edit the envelope freely.

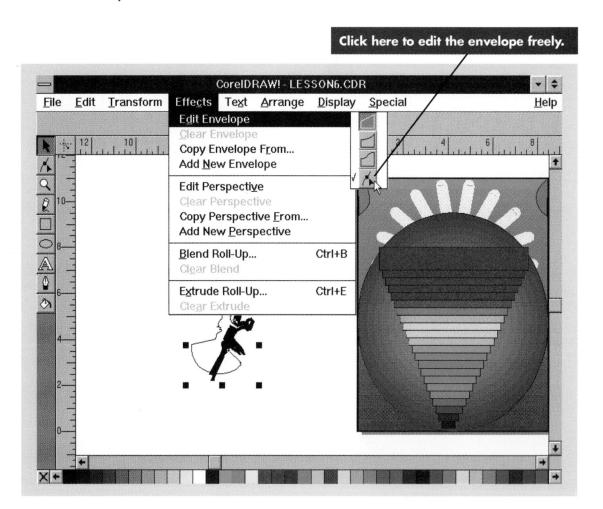

Click here to edit the envelope freely.

A red dotted line with nodes is displayed around the object. The Shape tool is automatically selected.

7. Drag a node in or out to change the shape of the object.

You can drag as many nodes as you like to change the shape of the dancers in different ways. You can also use Stretch and Mirror to reverse the image.

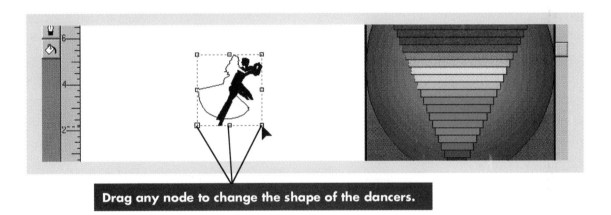

Drag any node to change the shape of the dancers.

8. Click the Pick tool.

9. Repeat steps 3 through 7 until you have five dancing couples, each a little different, off to the side of the page.

Aligning Objects

Now, you'll move the dancing couples to the bottom of the page and arrange them.

1. Click the Pick tool.

2. Drag each object to the bottom of the page.

Quick&Easy

Place the first object to the left in the position that you want it to stay in, and then you can reposition the others based on its location.

3. Press **Shift** and click each object, but click the dancers on the left last.

The objects will be aligned based on the last object you select.

4. Pull down the Arrange menu and choose Align.

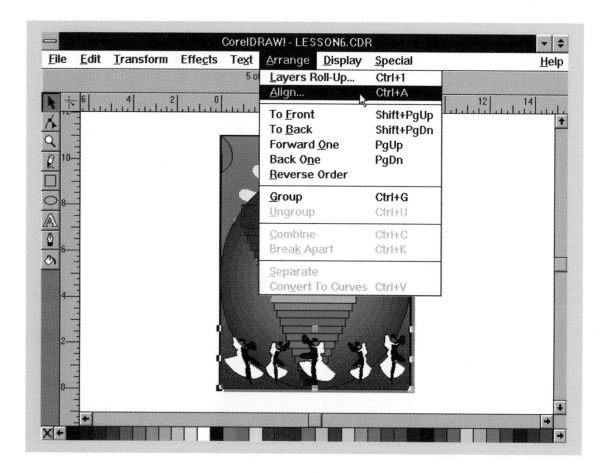

The Align dialog box is displayed.

5. Under Vertically, select Bottom.

6. Click OK.

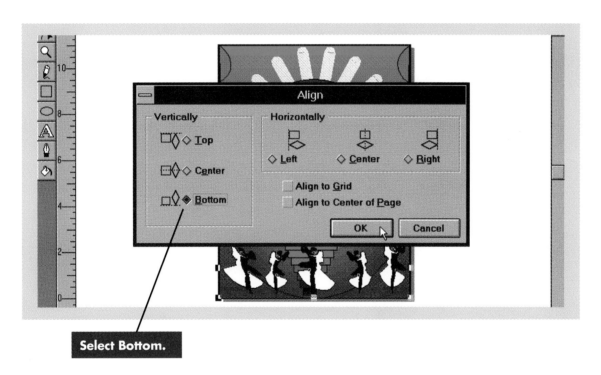

Select Bottom.

The objects will be aligned so that each is the same distance from the bottom of the page.

Finishing Touches

You'll notice that in our drawing, we added text in three different places, and one more rectangle to finish the lesson. You should be pretty good at text and rectangles by now, so we won't repeat the steps here.

And of course, before you quit CorelDRAW, don't forget to save and print your creation.

● **Note** How a radial fill looks when printed depends on whether you are using a PostScript or non-PostScript printer and the number of fountain stripes specified in the Print Options dialog box. See Lesson 5 for more information about printing and print options.

Managing and Printing Files and Graphics

Although you've been printing the drawings you've created, there are some additional printing capabilities we haven't tried yet. In this lesson, you'll learn how to benefit from some of the available print options and how to save a file for a service bureau. You'll also try some techniques in file importing and exporting and in using the Clipboard.

Using Print Options

Begin this lesson by opening the file you created in Lesson 6. The drawing included radial fills, so it is a good sample for this lesson.

1. Pull down the File menu and choose Open.

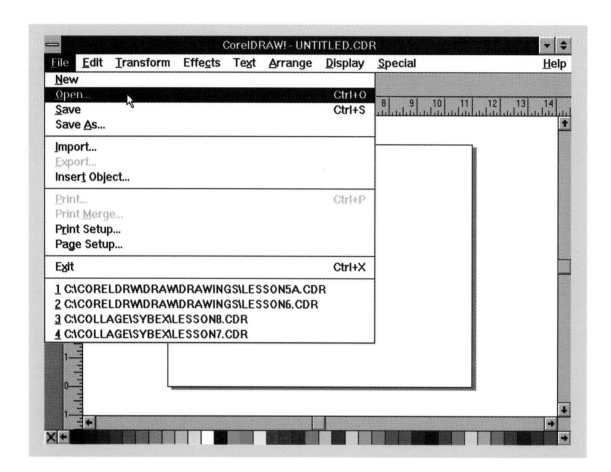

The Open Drawing dialog box is displayed.

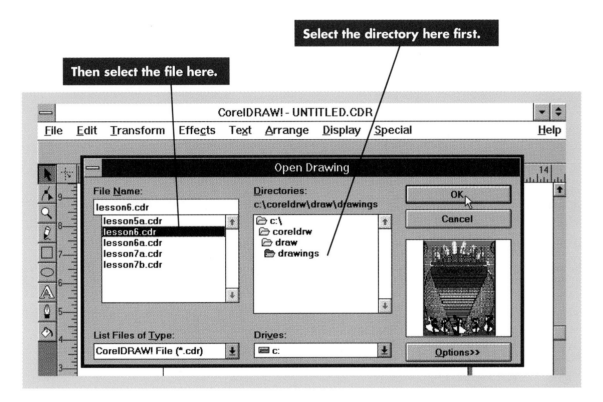

Select the directory here first.

Then select the file here.

2. In the Directories list box, double-click the directory where you've been saving your files. If you aren't sure, try the **draw** directory in **coreldrw** first.

3. Double-click **lesson6.cdr** in the File Name list box.

Now try changing the options CorelDRAW uses when you print at your own printer.

● Note Some of the printing options will be unavailable if the printer you have installed is not a PostScript printer.

1. Pull down the File menu and choose Print.

Quick&Easy

The Print Options dialog box is displayed.

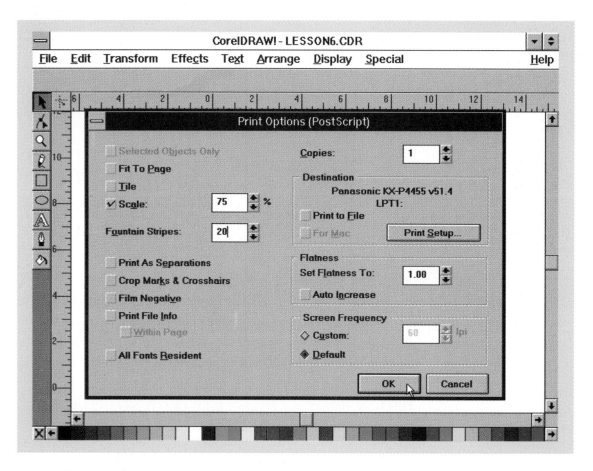

2. Check Scale and enter **75%** in the Scale text box.

This will reduce the size of the drawing, and also help speed up the printing. When you are printing for your own use in order to see a work in progress, this will save some time. It is also useful for proofing a drawing on a page size larger than your printer can handle.

3. Decrease the number of Fountain Stripes to **20**.

Fountain Stripes determines how many stripes a PostScript printer will print for each fountain fill in a drawing. Decreasing this number will increase the printing speed, but decrease the quality of your output.

4. Click OK.

The Printing File dialog box is displayed.

Printing to a File

Next, you'll prepare a file for printing from another computer or for delivery to a service bureau.

> **● Note** To print at a service bureau, you'll need to select the correct printer, based on the equipment the service bureau has. You can install and select another printer using the Windows Control Panel. Refer to the *Microsoft Windows User's Guide* for more information.

1. Pull down the File menu and choose Print. The Print dialog box is displayed.

2. Check Print to File.

3. Click OK.

The Print To File dialog box is displayed.

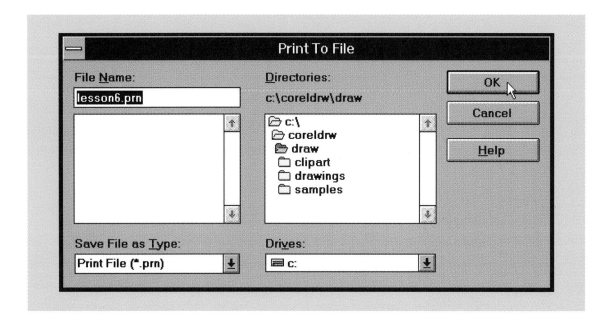

CorelDRAW automatically assigns a .PRN extension when it prints to
a file. The file name **lesson6.prn** is shown in the File Name text box.

4. Click OK.

The options dialog box for your printer is displayed. You do not need
to change the options in this box.

5. Click OK.

Your drawing is printed to a file named **lesson6.prn**. This file can be
printed from another computer or delivered to a service bureau for
printing.

Exporting a File

You'll probably want to include some of your drawings in documents you were creating in another application, for example a desktop publishing application. You'll need to save your drawings in a file format that is compatible with the other application. The Export command lets you do that.

1. Pull down the File menu and choose Export.

The Export File dialog box is displayed.

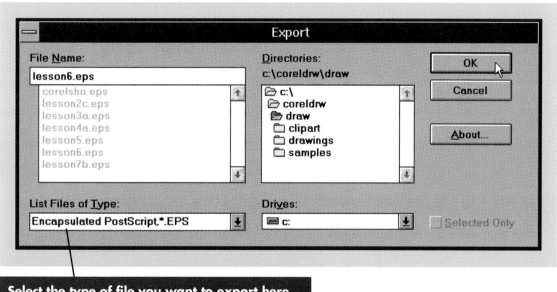

Select the type of file you want to export here.

2. Open the List Files of Type box and select Encapsulated Postscript,*.EPS.

3. Type the file name **lesson6.eps** in the File Name text box.

4. Click OK.

The Export EPS dialog box is displayed.

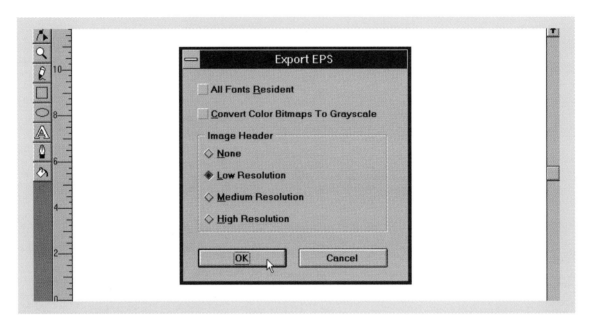

5. Select Low Resolution under Image Header.

This will allow you to see the image when you import your drawing into another application.

6. Click OK.

You'll see a dialog box that tells you CorelDRAW is exporting the file. You can open the file in any application that imports EPS files.

Importing a File

You've already imported clip art files into a CorelDRAW drawing. Now you'll import a TIF file. Begin with a new drawing page.

1. Pull down the File menu and choose New.

If you've made changes to **lesson6.cdr**, you'll be prompted to save the changes.

2. Pull down the File menu and choose Import.

The Import dialog box is displayed.

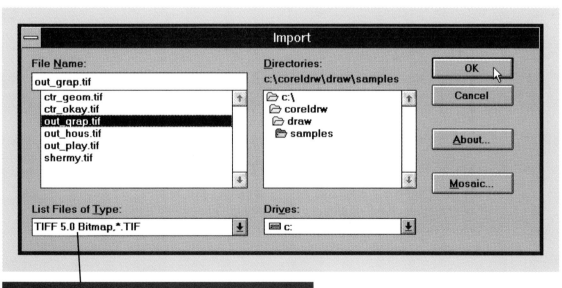

Select the type of file you want to import here.

3. Open the List Files of Type box and select TIFF 5.0 Bitmap,*.TIF.

4. In the Directories list box, double-click **coreldrw**, double-click **draw**, then double-click **samples**.

5. In the File Name list box, click **out_grap.tif**.

6. Click OK.

You'll see a dialog box that tells you CorelDRAW is importing the file. Then the file is included on your page and you can work with it as you do any other object.

To change the color of the grapes to purple:

1. Click the Outline tool.

2. In the Outline flyout menu, click the Color Wheel.

The Outline Color dialog box is displayed. The current color is 100% Black.

3. Use the scroll bars to change the color to **45%** Magenta, **20%** Yellow and **55%** Black.

4. Click OK.

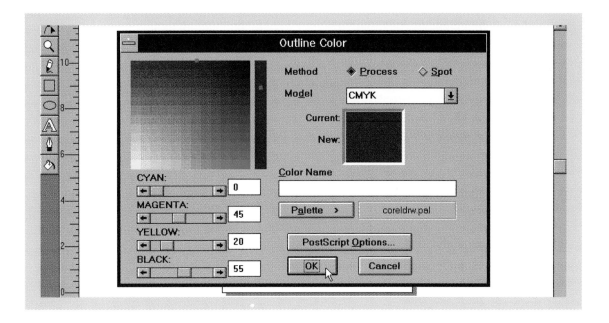

Copying with the Clipboard

If you had drawn one or more objects in one drawing and wanted to include them in another drawing, you could easily do this through the Windows Clipboard. Since you have a bunch of grapes on your page right now, let's copy them to one of your earlier drawings.

1. Pull down the Edit menu and choose Copy.

2. Pull down the File menu and select one of the files shown at the bottom. We selected **lesson5.cdr**.

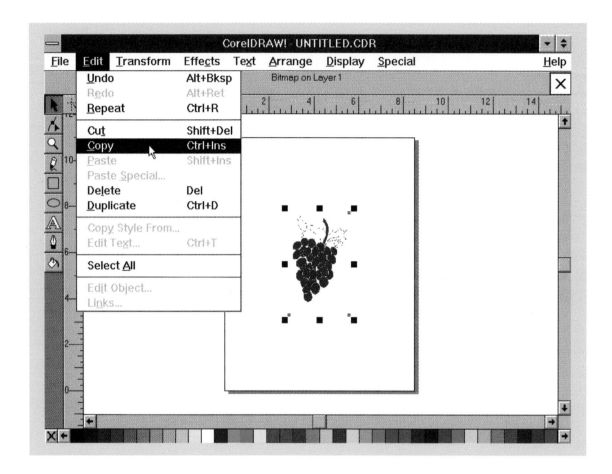

3. Click No when you see the Save Current Changes? prompt.

4. Pull down the Edit menu and choose Paste.

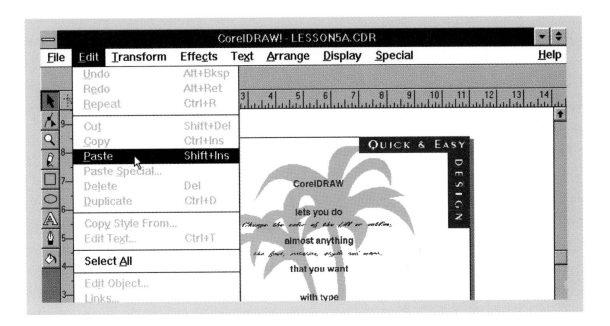

5. If you can't see the grapes, pull down the Arrange menu and choose To Front.

With CorelDRAW, you can make grapes grow from palm trees.

You can copy any objects from one drawing to another by selecting them, choosing Copy, then choosing Paste when you have the destination displayed on the drawing page.

Finishing Up

You can quit CorelDRAW now if you like, since this is the last lesson on CorelDRAW. Or you may want to try out some of the techniques you've learned before you move on to Part II.

When you are finished, pull down the File menu and choose Exit.

Learning Additional Applications

Now that you know how to draw and design, you are probably eager to get started with the other Corel applications. In Part Two, you'll learn how to:

- Design and enhance drawings and other images with Corel-PHOTO-PAINT.

- Create and produce an effective on-screen video presentation with CorelSHOW.

- Automatically generate and then build better-looking charts with CorelCHART.

Painting with CorelPHOTO-PAINT

In this lesson, you'll learn the basics of Corel-PHOTO-PAINT and use many of its tools to *paint* a picture you begin in CorelDRAW. In order to speed up the learning process and quickly begin working in CorelPHOTO-PAINT, you'll create a drawing using clip art and some of CorelDRAW's tools, then export it to Corel-PHOTO-PAINT.

> **● Note** CorelPHOTO-PAINT does not include as many import filters as CorelDRAW. For example, you cannot import CorelDRAW's clip art files, which have a .CDR extension, directly into CorelPHOTO-PAINT. However, you can import them into CorelDRAW and then save your drawing as a CorelPHOTO-PAINT file. That's one reason to begin in CorelDRAW.

Preliminary Steps

> **● Note** Before you begin the lesson, close all open and minimized applications so that you'll have the maximum amount of memory available to work with CorelPHOTO-PAINT's tools.

Begin by starting CorelDRAW and creating a simple drawing with clip art, shapes, and text. You can use any of the clip art that you installed with CorelDRAW, or art from other sources, for example:

- The TIFF files in the **coreldrw\draw\samples** directory or any scanned image that has the extension .TIF.

- The Windows bitmap files included in the **windows** directory that have the extension .BMP.

Putting Objects Together

First, start CorelDRAW.

1. Double-click the CorelDRAW icon in the Corel Graphics group window.

2. Pull down the File menu and choose Import.

The Import dialog box is displayed.

3. Open the List Files of Type box and select the type of file you want to import.

If you need additional instructions on how to import files, refer to Lesson 4.

Repeat the process until you have a simple drawing with a few different objects. Then add some shapes and text. Our drawing includes two different types of buildings, a person, some rectangles, and text.

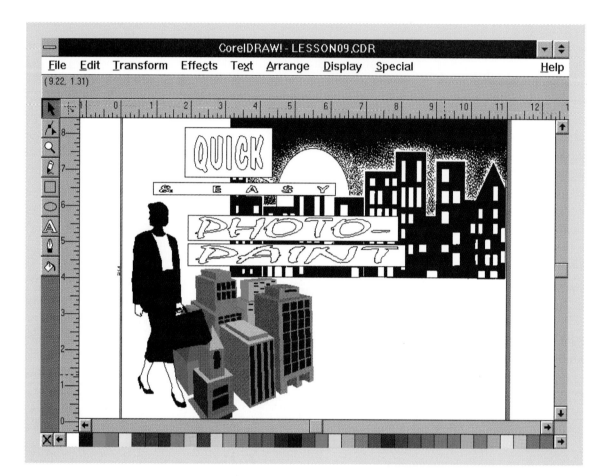

Exporting a File to CorelPHOTO-PAINT

Try to create a drawing with the same types of elements as ours, so you can apply the techniques in the lesson. But feel free to create something you like; your drawing does not have to be identical to ours. When you are satisfied with it, you are ready to move on to CorelPHOTO-PAINT.

1. Pull down the File menu and choose Export. The Export File dialog box is displayed.

2. Open the List Files of Type box and select CorelPHOTO-
PAINT, *.PCX;*.PCC.

3. Type the file name **lesson08.pcx** in the File Name text box.

4. Click OK.

The Bitmap Export dialog box is displayed.

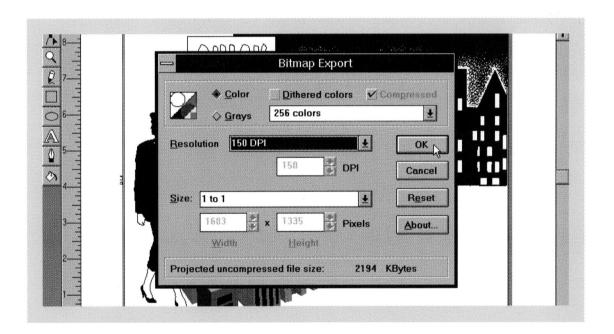

5. Select Color

6. In the drop-down list-box, select **256** colors.

7. In the Resolution drop-down list-box, select **150 DPI**.

The higher the resolution, the larger the file size. The projected file size is shown at the bottom of this list box. If you want to conserve hard disk space, you can select a lower resolution.

8. In the Size drop-down list box, select 1 to 1.

9. Click OK.

You'll see a dialog box that tells you CorelDRAW is exporting the file.

10. When this dialog box closes, pull down the File menu and choose Exit.

11. When prompted to save the file, select Yes and name the file **lesson08.cdr**.

You'll have a copy of the file saved in case you want to modify it later.

Getting Started

1. Double-click the CorelPHOTO-PAINT icon in the Corel Graphics group window.

The CorelPHOTO-PAINT window is opened.

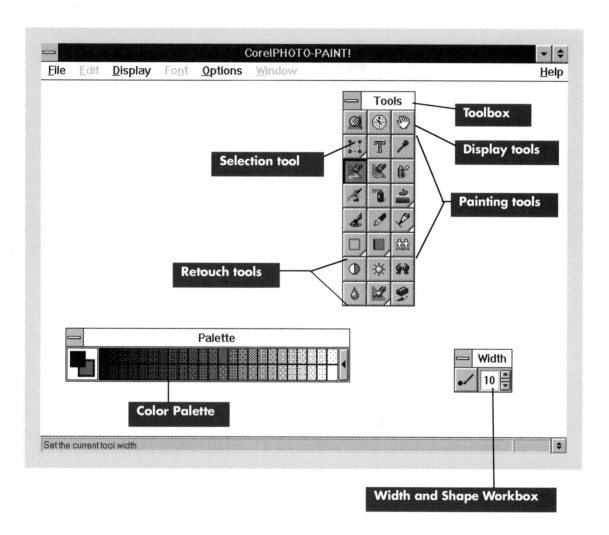

The main items in the window, in addition to the standard Window elements, are the Toolbox, Color Palette, and Width and Shape workbox. The Toolbox looks different from the one you used in CorelDRAW and contains more tools. Fortunately, you don't have to remember which tool is which because as you point to each tool, its name is shown at the bottom of the screen. Try it now:

2. Slowly move the mouse pointer over each tool, and watch the bottom of the window.

Now let's start working on the file you created.

1. Pull down the File menu and choose Open.

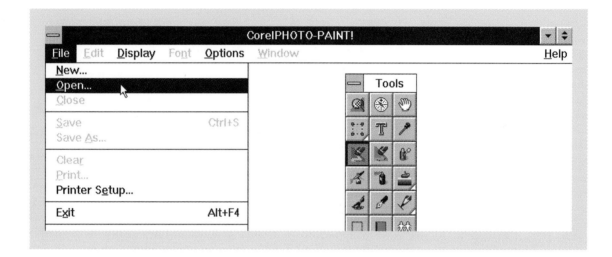

The Load a Picture from Disk dialog box is displayed.

2. Open the List Files of Type box and select All images.

3. In the Directories list box, double-click the directory where you've been saving your files.

4. Click the file name **lesson08.pcx** in the File Name list box.

5. Click OK.

The picture you started in CorelDRAW is displayed in a Corel-PHOTO-PAINT *picture window.* You can make many additions and modifications to the picture using the tools in the Toolbox.

Using Fill Tools

The first addition you'll make is color—to the background and to some of the objects. Begin by using a gradient fill for some of the rectangles.

1. Click and hold the right corner of the Flood Fill tool to open the Fill flyout menu; then select the Gradient Fill tool, which is on the right.

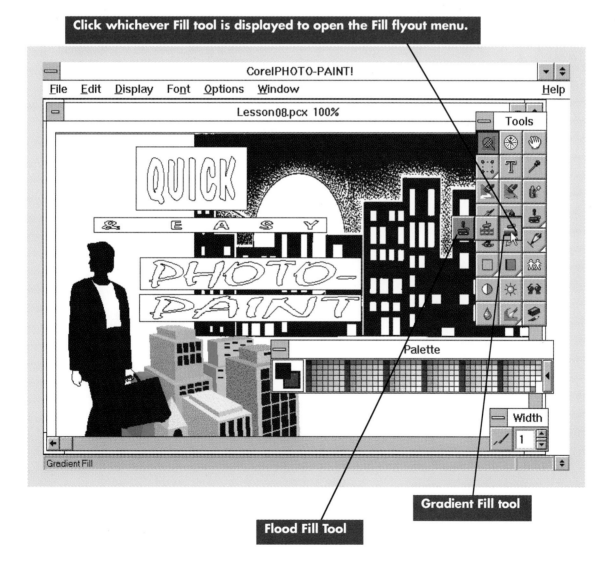

Click whichever Fill tool is displayed to open the Fill flyout menu.

Gradient Fill tool

Flood Fill Tool

2. Pull down the Options menu and choose Gradient Type.

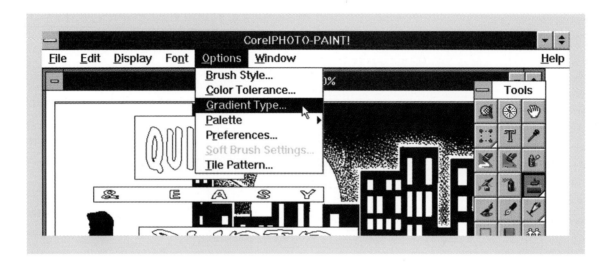

A dialog box is displayed with three styles for the effect.

3. Click Vertical.

4. Click OK to close the dialog box.

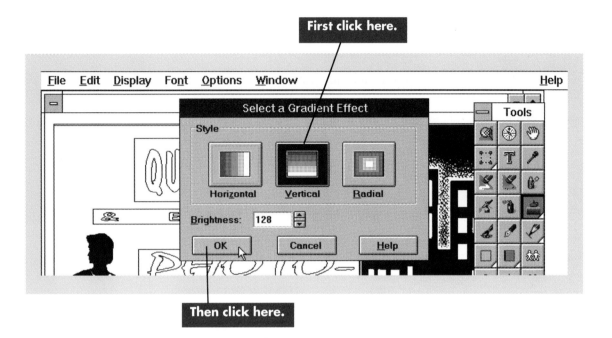

Now choose the colors for the fill from the color palette. You'll choose a secondary color and a background color for the fill. The color of the fill is blended from the secondary to the background color.

• Note Later, you'll also select a primary color to be used for other effects.

1. Click the right mouse button anywhere in the palette to select the secondary color.

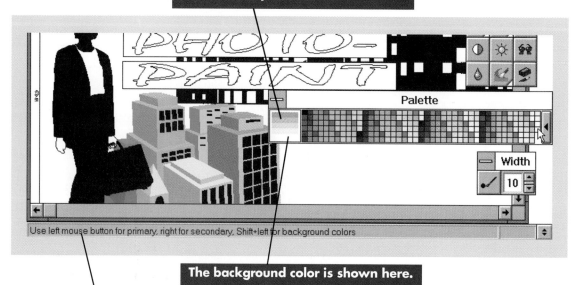

The secondary color is shown here.

Palette

Width

10

Use left mouse button for primary, right for secondary, Shift+left for background colors

The background color is shown here.

A reminder is shown here.

2. Press **Shift** and click the left mouse button in the palette to select the background color.

3. Move the Gradient Fill tool to the first rectangle you want to fill and click.

The rectangle is filled with the gradient fill. The tool is still active, so if you aren't happy with the effect:

1. Pull down the Edit menu and choose Undo Gradient Fill.

Now, go back to the palette and select different colors.

2. Click the right mouse button in the palette to select the secondary color.

3. Press **Shift** and click the left mouse button in the palette to select the background color.

We also used a vertical gradient fill to add color to the windows in the buildings on the right. Apply this fill to any areas you want, changing the colors.

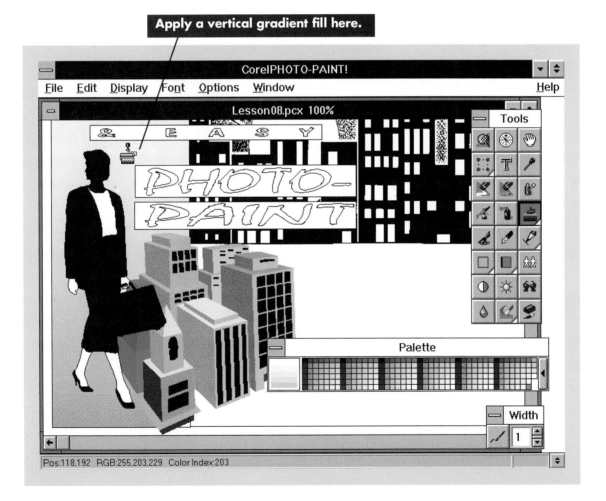

Apply a vertical gradient fill here.

When you're finished, use the horizontal fill for the area behind the text.

1. Pull down the Options menu and choose Gradient Type.

2. Click Horizontal.

3. Click OK to close the dialog box.

Now choose the secondary and background colors for the fill and apply them to the rectangles behind the text. We also used a radial fill to fill in the moon behind the buildings.

Next, use the Flood Fill tool to fill in the letters with a solid color.

1. Click and hold the right corner of the Fill tool to open the Fill flyout menu, then select the Flood Fill tool, which is on the left. The Flood Fill tool applies the primary color.

2. Click the left mouse button in the palette to select the primary color.

3. Make sure the *drop* on the Flood Fill tool is inside the letter **P** in **PHOTO**, and click.

Make sure the *drop* on the Flood Fill tool is inside the area you want to fill.

The letter is filled with the primary color. Repeat the process to fill in all the letters, changing the color if you wish. If you are unhappy with the effect:

4. Pull down the Edit menu and choose Undo Flood Fill.

Apply the Flood Fill tool to other areas that are still without color, or to change the color of any areas. We also used the Flood Fill tool to fill in the ground in our picture.

Zooming In

You'll probably want to magnify an area when you are creating most of the effects, so you can work in a more detailed way.

1. Click the Zoom tool.

2. Point to the area you want to magnify and click the left mouse button.

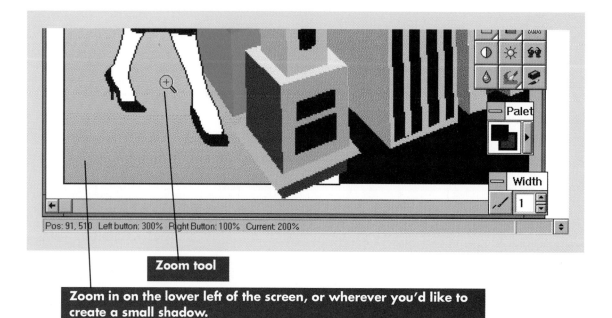

Zoom tool

Zoom in on the lower left of the screen, or wherever you'd like to create a small shadow.

Clicking the left mouse button magnifies the picture to 200% and shows you the area you selected. If the area is still not magnified enough:

3. Point to the area and click again.

Clicking again magnifies the area to 300%. Try working in magnified view for a while. To return to normal view later:

4. Double-click the Zoom tool.

Changing the Palette

In addition to the palette that is displayed when you launch Corel-PHOTO-PAINT, there are a number of others you can display and work from to quickly provide more diversity.

1. Pull down the Options menu and choose Palette.

2. Choose Open Palette from the menu.

The Load a Palette from Disk dialog box is displayed.

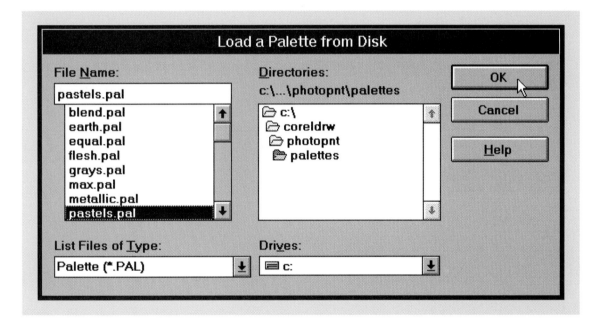

3. In the Directories list box, double-click the **coreldraw\photopnt\palettes** directory.

4. Double-click any file in the File Name list box.

5. Choose OK.

The new palette is displayed. If you aren't satisfied with it, repeat the steps to select another one.

Spray Painting an Area

Once you have filled in many of the larger areas, you'll want to soften the look of some fills. For example, we used the Spraycan tool to place a shadow behind the woman's legs and add a more interesting and uneven look to the ground.

1. Click the Spraycan tool. The Spraycan applies the primary color.

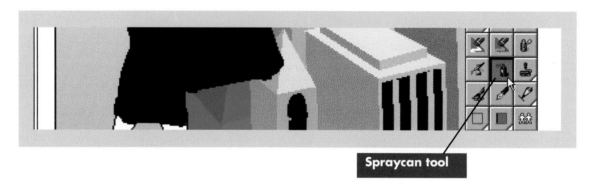

Spraycan tool

2. Click the left mouse button in the palette to select the primary color.

Now change the size and shape of the brush.

3. Pull down the Options menu and choose Brush Style. The Select a Brush Style dialog box is displayed.

4. Click a brush style you'd like to try. For the shadow, the round style might be best.

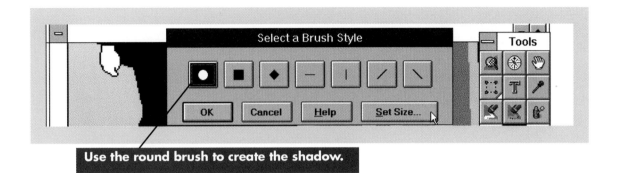

Use the round brush to create the shadow.

5. Choose Set Size.

The Set the Drawing Width dialog box is displayed; here you can set the width of the brush and the units in which it is measured.

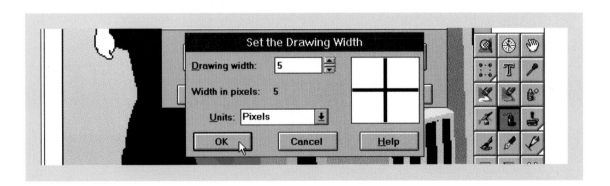

6. Set the size to 5 pixels to start.

7. Choose OK to close the Set the Drawing Width dialog box.

8. Choose OK to close the Select a Brush Style dialog box.

9. Drag the pointer in the area behind the woman's legs to create a shadow effect.

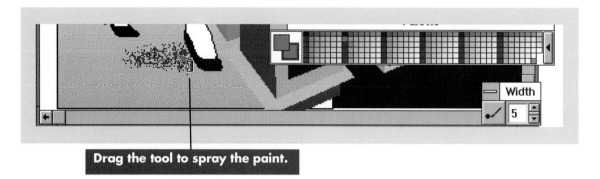

Drag the tool to spray the paint.

If you make a mistake, you can use the Local Undo tool to erase a small area.

1. Click the Local Undo tool.

2. Drag the pointer over the area you want to eliminate.

Local Undo tool

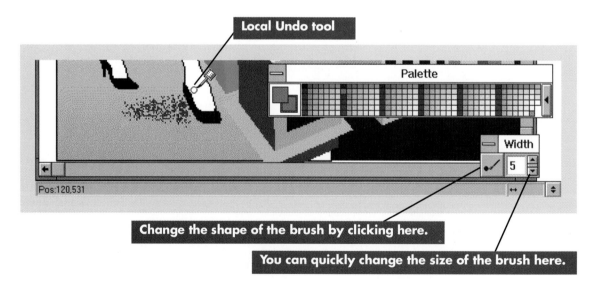

Change the shape of the brush by clicking here.

You can quickly change the size of the brush here.

The sprayed-on color is removed and the background color remains.

We used the Spraycan tool to add some texture to the ground, spraying a red color over the black ground and adding more blue to the sky. You may want to change the shape and size of the brush as well as its color, depending on what you are spraying. If you want to change the size but not the shape, you can quickly do that with the Width and Shape workbox.

Next, we'll add some larger, more visible stars to the sky.

1. Click the Pen tool.

2. Click in the palette to change the primary color.

3. If necessary, change the brush shape and width.

4. Click in the sky wherever you want to add stars.

Creating Objects

You may have noticed that there are some blank areas in the drawing that need more than color—they need objects. There are several methods for adding objects. First, you'll draw an object with the Polygon tool between the words **Easy** and **PHOTO**.

1. Click and hold the right corner of the Filled Box tool to open the flyout menu; then select the Filled Polygon tool, which is on the right.

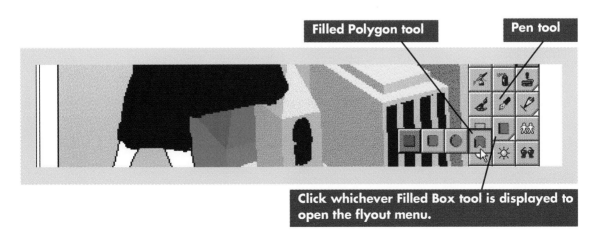

Filled Polygon tool

Pen tool

Click whichever Filled Box tool is displayed to open the flyout menu.

2. Click to begin the shape, then click at each angle to draw a triangle.

3. When you've connected the last line, double-click inside the triangle, and it will be filled with the primary color.

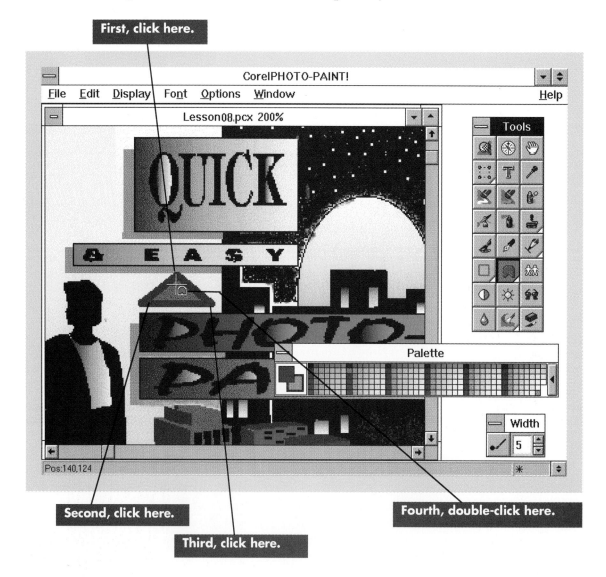

First, click here.

Second, click here.

Third, click here.

Fourth, double-click here.

The Filled Polygon tool lets you create multisided objects with this "connect-the-dots" method. You can change the color of the triangle with any of the Fill tools before you go on.

Selecting and Copying Objects

It's as easy to duplicate a rectangular object in CorelPHOTO-PAINT as it is in CorelDRAW. You can quickly increase the amount of buildings on the right by copying and pasting them.

1. Click the Box Selection tool.

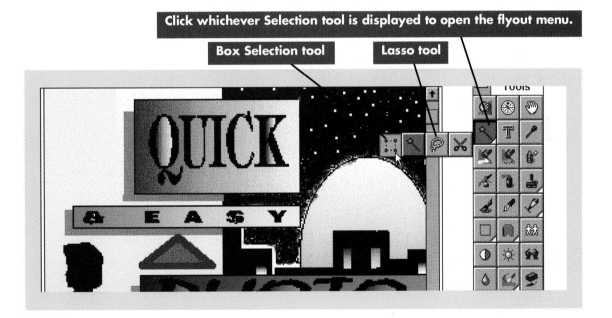

Select the two buildings on the left.

2. Drag the pointer from the top left to the bottom right of the buildings and release the mouse button.

QuickEasy

The buildings are surrounded by a rectangle.

3. Pull down the Edit menu and choose Copy. The area is
copied to the Windows Clipboard.

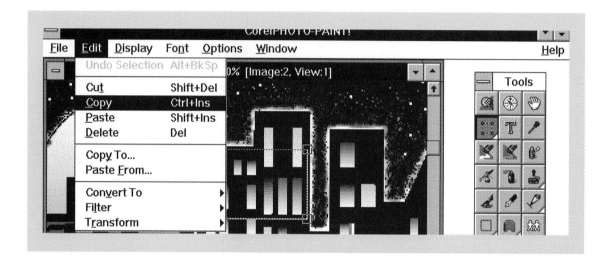

4. Pull down the Edit menu again and choose Paste. The area
is pasted to the top left of the window and is selected.

5. Drag the area to the front of the buildings. It is still selected.

6. Drag any corner to increase the size of the buildings slightly.

Because the new buildings are being placed in front, you'll want them
to be slightly larger to maintain a proportional look.

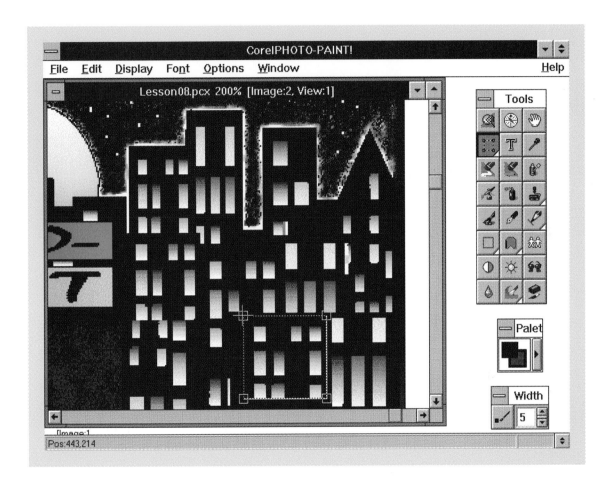

7. Repeat steps 4 through 6 to paste additional buildings.

To copy the building with the pointed roof, use the Lasso tool, which lets you define an irregular shape or area.

1. Click and hold the right corner of the Box Selection tool to open the flyout menu; then select the Lasso tool.

2. Use the pointer to draw a line around the area in order to define it. Once the area is defined, it is selected.

3. Use Copy and Paste to duplicate it.

Painting Lines

To make the buildings' outlines stand out, we painted lines around them with the Line tool. Try adding lines to help define objects.

1. Click the Line tool.

2. Select the color, width, and shape of the line.

3. Hold down the Shift key and click at the line's starting point, then drag and click at the line's ending point. Holding down the Shift key constrains the angle of the line so that it is straight.

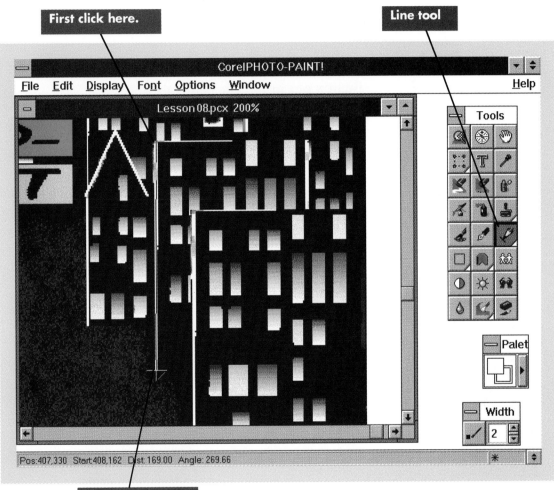

First click here.

Line tool

Then click here.

Finishing Touches

Add any additional objects you'd like to your painting and change any colors or fills you aren't satisfied with. When you are done, save and print it.

To save it and keep your original:

1. Pull down the File menu and choose Save As.

2. Open the List Files of Type box and select ZSoft Image (*.PCX).

3. Type the file name **final08.pcx** in the File Name text box.

4. Click OK.

To print it:

1. Pull down the File menu and choose Print.

The Print dialog box is displayed.

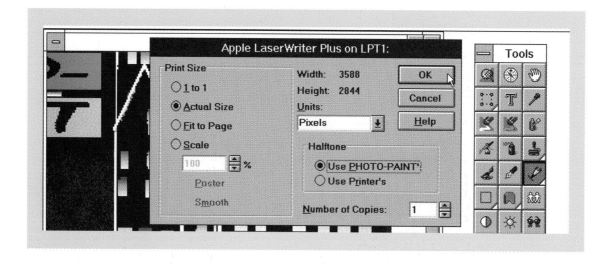

2. Under Print Size, select Actual Size. Or, if your image is too large to print at your printer, select Print to Page or select Scale and, in the Scale text box, enter a percentage that is smaller than a full page.

3. If you are printing a color image on a black and white printer, select Use PHOTO-PAINT's under Halftone.

4. Click OK.

The Printing File dialog box is displayed and your painting is printed.

Here's how our finished painting looked.

Creating a Presentation with CorelSHOW

W ith CorelSHOW you can put together a presentation that's made up of drawings, charts, texts, and animations created in other applications. The presentation can be in the form of a brochure, slide show, or a screen show that plays on your computer. In this lesson, you'll create a screen show using files CorelDRAW and CorelCHART files.

Getting Started

1. If the Corel Graphics group window is not open, double-click the Corel Graphics icon at the bottom of the Program Manager window.

2. To start CorelSHOW, double-click the CorelSHOW icon in the Corel Graphics group window.

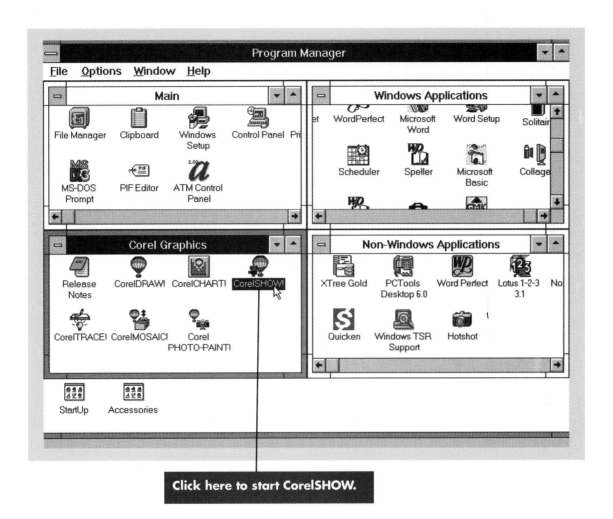

Click here to start CorelSHOW.

The Welcome to CorelSHOW dialog box is shown first. You'll need to make some decisions right away, but they can be changed later if necessary.

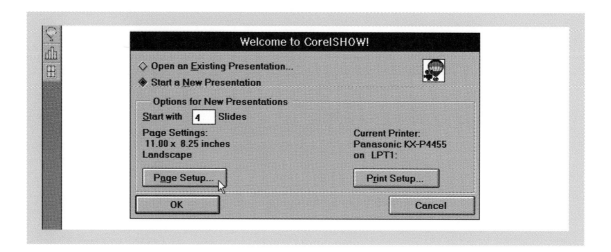

3. Select Start a New Presentation.

4. In the Start with Slides box, enter **4**.

5. Choose Page Setup.

The Page Setup dialog box is shown.

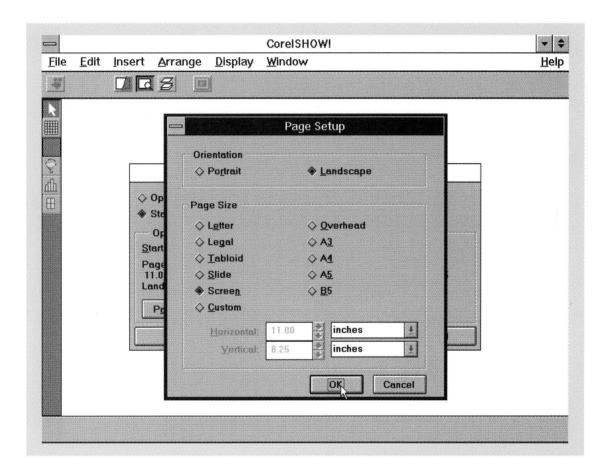

6. Under Orientation, select Landscape.

7. Under Page Size, select Screen.

8. Choose OK in the Page Setup dialog box.

9. Choose OK in the Welcome dialog box.

Quick Easy

You'll see the CorelSHOW application window. On the left, you'll see the tools that let you *link* files to CorelSHOW. When you link files, they are included in the presentation, but remain separate files.

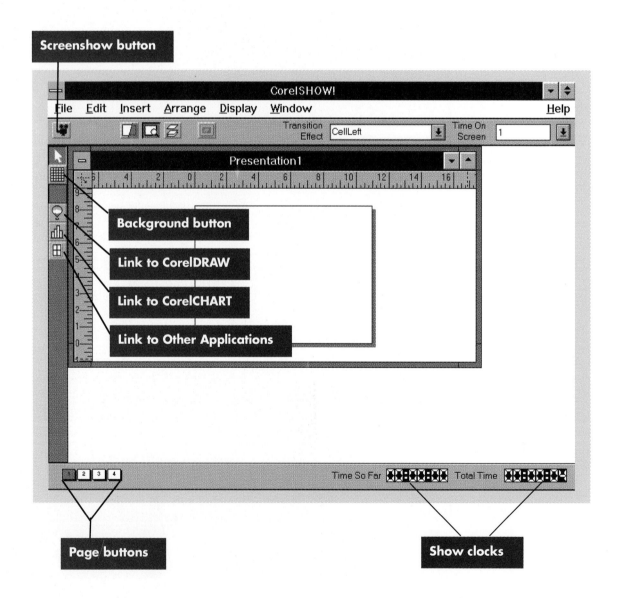

Screenshow button

Background button

Link to CorelDRAW

Link to CorelCHART

Link to Other Applications

Page buttons

Show clocks

Including a CorelDRAW File

Slide View is currently active. This means that one slide is displayed and you can work with its contents. Slide View is where you'll do most of the work with slides. The Presentation1 window is blank.

1. Click the maximize button in the Presentation1 window so that you have a larger area to work in.

2. Click the minimize button in the top-right corner of the CorelSHOW window.

3. To start CorelDRAW, double-click the CorelDRAW icon in the Corel Graphics group window.

4. Pull down the File menu and choose Open.

5. In the Open Drawing dialog box, select any drawing you've created or any CorelDRAW sample drawing (with the file extension **.cdr**) you'd like to use; then click OK.

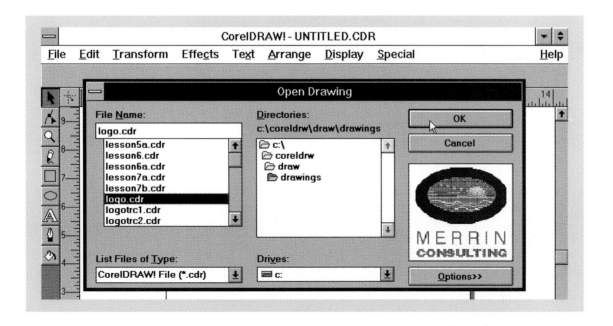

The file you selected is displayed on your screen.

6. Pull down the Edit menu and choose Select All.

A selection box surrounds the drawing.

7. Pull down the Edit menu again and choose Copy.

Your drawing is copied to the Windows Clipboard.

● Note If you need to refresh your memory on copying and pasting an object using the Windows Clipboard, refer to Lesson 7.

8. Click the minimize button in the top-right corner of the CorelDRAW window.

9. Double-click the CorelSHOW minimized icon.

10. Pull down the Edit menu in CorelSHOW and choose Paste.

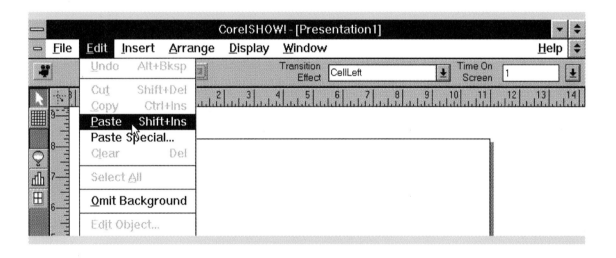

The drawing is probably larger than the Presentation window.

11. Pull down the Arrange menu and choose Fit Object To Page.

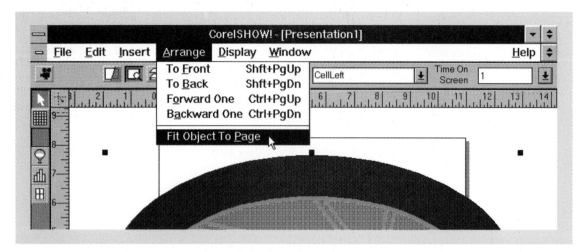

12. Now use the sizing handles to drag the object in to about
half the slide, so you'll have room for some text on the bottom.

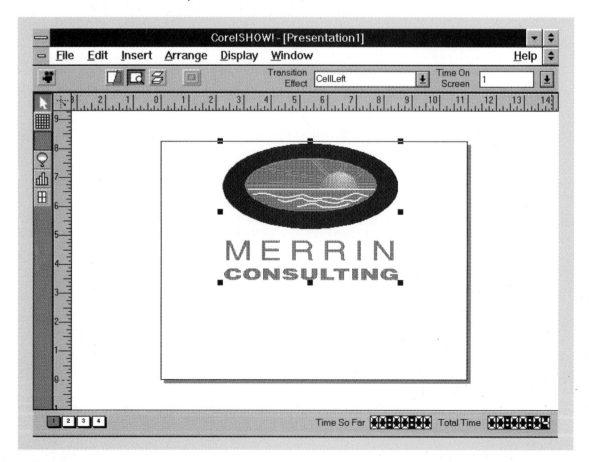

Adding Text to a Page

You can go back to CorelDRAW again to create some text and then paste it on this first slide. There is a different technique for including something you haven't created yet.

1. Click the CorelDRAW tool.

2. Use the cursor to draw a rectangle on the bottom of the slide.

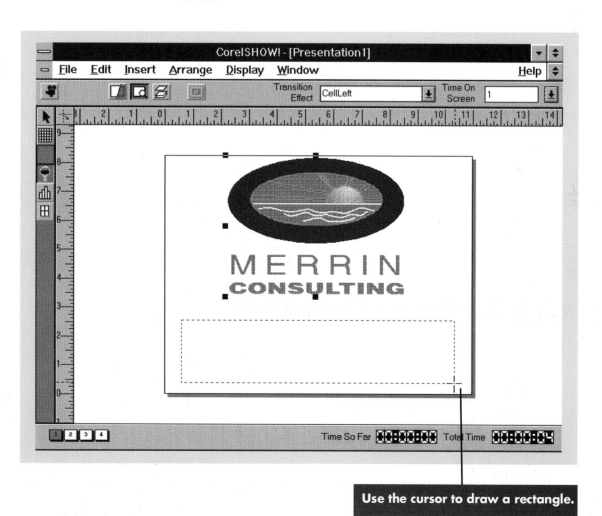

Use the cursor to draw a rectangle.

Once you release the mouse button, the CorelDRAW window is opened again.

3. Use the Text tool to create some text. If you are creating a presentation similar to ours, type **A Company with a Proven Track Record**.

4. Click the Pick tool and change the size and color of the text. Look back at Lesson 5 if you've forgotten how to do this.

5. With the text still selected, pull down the Edit menu and choose Copy.

6. Click the minimize button in the top-right corner of the CorelDRAW window.

The CorelSHOW window was never minimized, so it is still on your screen.

7. Pull down the Edit menu again and choose Paste.

8. Drag the text in to fit below the drawing.

Your first slide is complete for now.

Saving Your Show

This is a good time to save your show.

1. Pull down the File menu and choose Save.

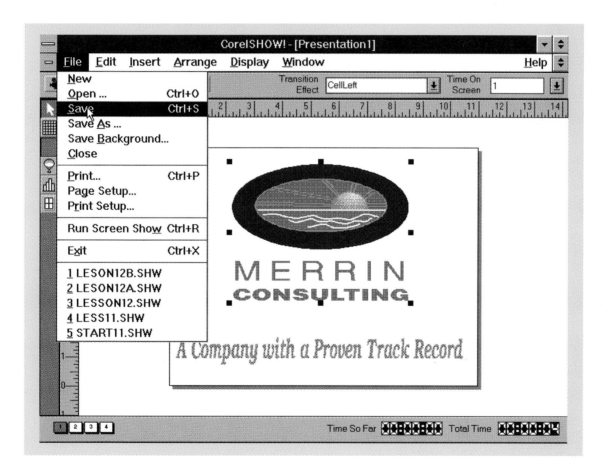

2. In the Save Presentation dialog box, enter the File Name **lesson09.shw**.

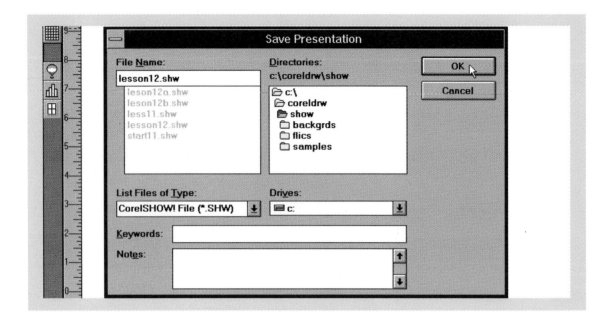

3. Choose OK.

Don't forget to save every so often as you go along.

Including a CorelCHART File

The preliminary work on the first slide is done, so let's move to the next slide and bring in a chart. (You'll learn to use CorelCHART in the final lesson of this book.) The steps are very similar.

1. Click the 2 in the bottom-left corner to display the second slide in the show, which is blank at the moment.

2. Click the minimize button in the top-right corner of the CorelSHOW window.

3. Double-click the CorelCHART icon in the Corel Graphics group window to start CorelCHART.

4. Pull down the File menu and choose Open.

5. In the Open Chart dialog box, select any file you'd like to include. There are a number of charts included in the SAMPLES directory.

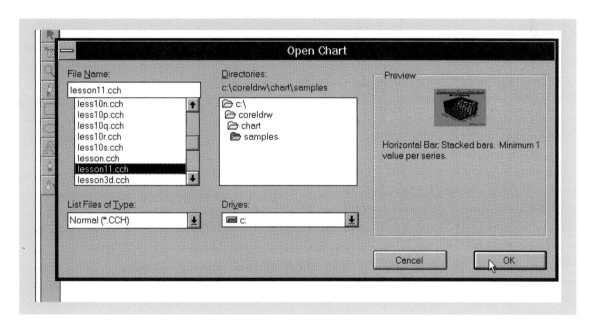

You can select any CorelCHART file (with the file extension **.cch**).

6. Choose OK.

The file you selected is on your screen.

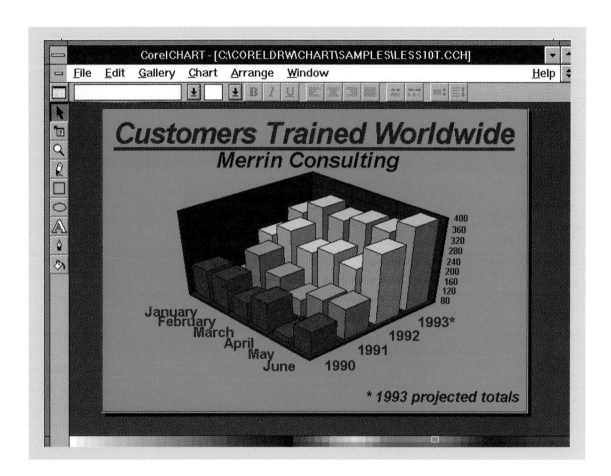

7. Pull down the Edit menu and choose Copy Chart.

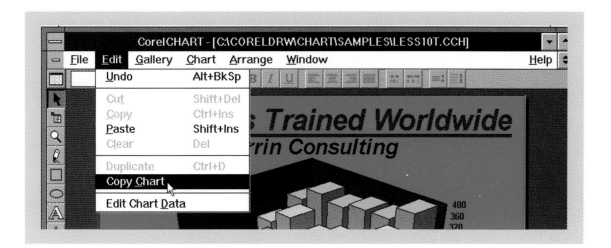

Your chart is copied to the Windows Clipboard.

8. Pull down the File menu and choose Exit.

Now go back to CorelSHOW.

1. Double-click the CorelSHOW minimized icon.

2. Pull down CorelSHOW's Edit menu again and choose Paste Special.

The Paste Special dialog box is displayed.

3. Select CorelCHART Chart.

4. Choose Paste.

5. Pull down the Arrange menu and choose Fit Object To Page.

You have the preliminary content for your second slide.

6. Pull down the File menu and choose Save.

Adding a Text Slide

Let's move to the next slide and add text only. By now, you can see how easy that will be.

1. Click the 3 in the bottom-left corner to display the third slide.

2. Click the CorelDRAW tool.

3. Use the cursor to draw a rectangle on the slide.

Once you release the mouse button, the CorelDRAW window is opened again.

4. Use the Text tool to create some text. If you are creating a presentation similar to ours, type **is proud to present**.

5. Click the Pick tool and modify the text.

6. With the text still selected, pull down the File menu and choose Exit & Return to CorelSHOW.

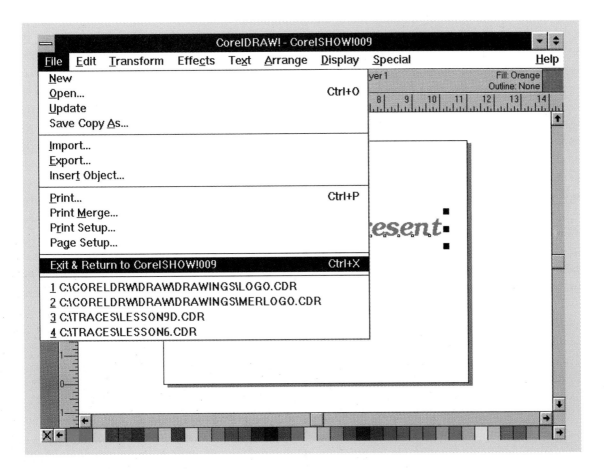

Quick & Easy

> **● Note** You'll also see a number, such as 009, at the end of the
> command. CorelSHOW assigns numbers as you include new
> objects in order to keep track of the objects and their locations.
> You do not have to memorize the numbers; you can always
> select an object by clicking it.

7. When you see the prompt **Update the embedded object?**,
choose Yes.

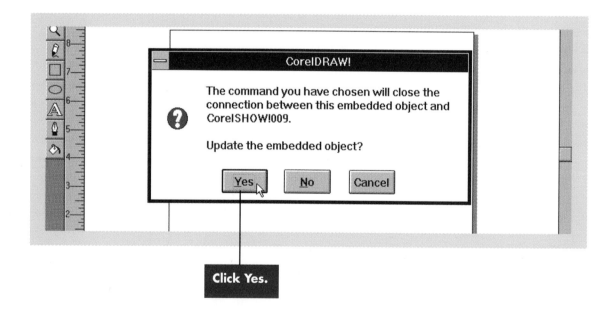

Click Yes.

You'll be back in CorelSHOW and see the text you created on slide
number 3.

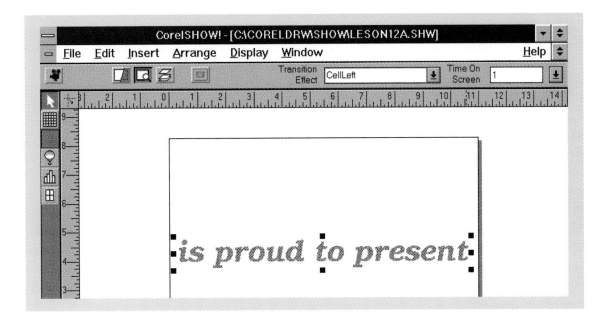

Adding a Final Drawing

You can quickly add the final drawing to slide number 4 using the Insert File command. We'll add a drawing we created in Lesson 6, with a few modifications.

Choose any drawing or chart you'd like to include in the last frame.

1. Click the 4 in the bottom-left corner to display slide number 4.

2. Pull down the Insert menu and choose File.

The Insert File dialog box is displayed.

Quick Easy

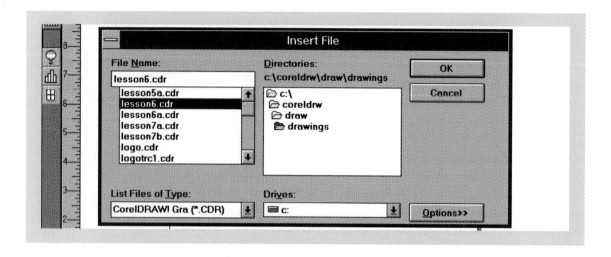

3. In the Insert File dialog box, select any CorelDRAW file you'd like to add to the current slide.

4. Choose OK.

5. Use the crosshair cursor to draw a frame on the slide.

The file is displayed on the slide.

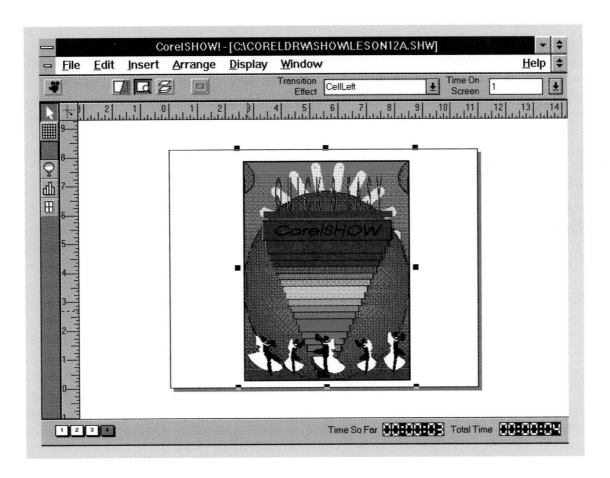

6. Pull down the File menu and choose Save.

Enhancing the Presentation

Now that you have four slides, there are several additional decisions to make:

- Do you want to enhance the show with an animation?

- What would you like in the background?

- How long do you want each slide to stay on the screen?

- What would you like to see between each slide?

- Should the show play automatically or not?

Adding Animation

Another enhancement you could make is the addition of animation
to this show. CorelSHOW includes some animations in the **samples**
subdirectory. First, you'll have to insert another slide, but that's easy to do.

1. Click the Slide Sorter View button to change the view.

You'll see a miniature view of each slide in order.

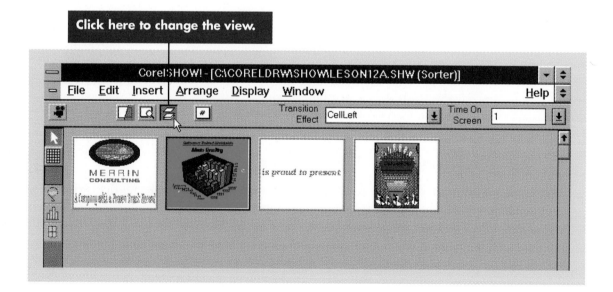

Click here to change the view.

2. Click the first slide.

3. Pull down the Insert menu and choose New Page.

The Insert New Page dialog box is displayed.

4. Select Before Current.

5. Choose OK.

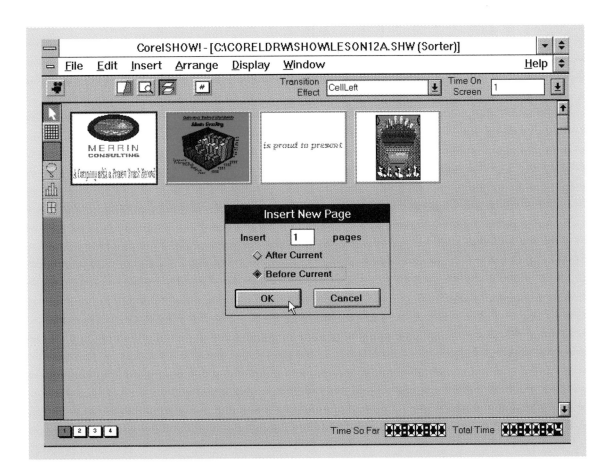

A blank slide is inserted at the beginning of the show. Now insert the
animation.

1. Pull down the Insert menu again and choose Animation.

The Insert Animation dialog box is displayed.

2. Open the List Files of Type box and select Autodesk
File (*.fli).

3. In the Directories list box, double-click **coreldrw**, double-
click **show**, then double-click **flics**.

4. In the File Name list box, click **nenwelc.fli**.

5. Drag the scroll bar to "play" the animation.

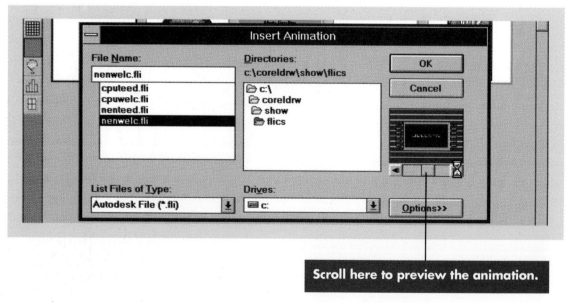

Scroll here to preview the animation.

6. Click OK.

Adding a Background

This is a good view to use when you select a background, because you can see how the background works with all the slides.

● Note The background won't be added to the animation slide.

1. Click the Background library tool. The Background library window opens.

2. Use the scroll bar to look through the backgrounds.

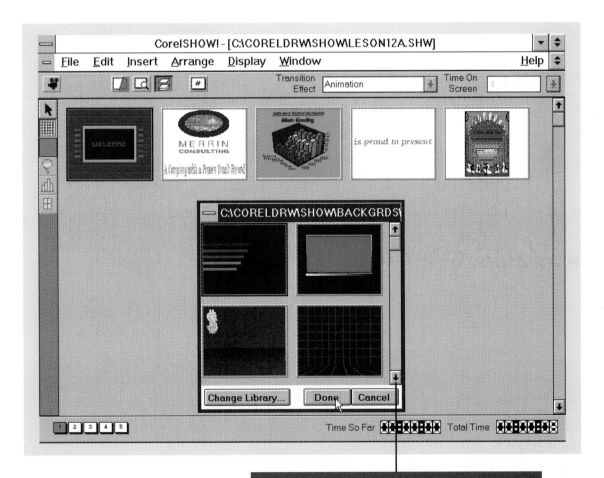

Scroll here to see the available backgrounds.

3. When you see one you'd like to try, click it. It will be added to each slide.

4. If you'd like to try another background, click it.

Continue trying backgrounds until you find one you like.

5. Then choose Done.

Setting the Playing Times

Here, you will decide how long each slide should stay on the screen and set the times accordingly.

● Note The animation time can be changed in the Insert Animation dialog box, but not here.

1. Click the second slide.

2. Open the Time On Screen list box and click the number of seconds you wish. We chose 5.

3. Click the third slide.

4. Open the Time On Screen list box again and click the number of seconds.

5. Repeat the steps for slides 4 and 5.

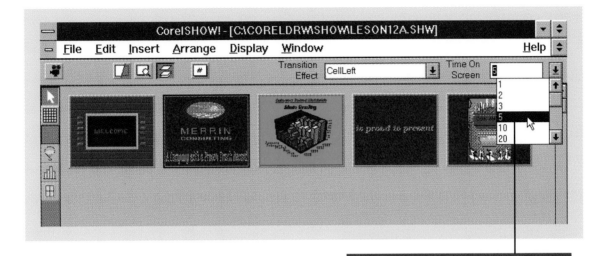

Click the number of seconds here.

You may want to keep slide 4, which has only text, on the screen for a shorter time and the last slide for a longer time than the other slides.

Now play your show to see how it's coming along.

1. Click the Screenshow button.

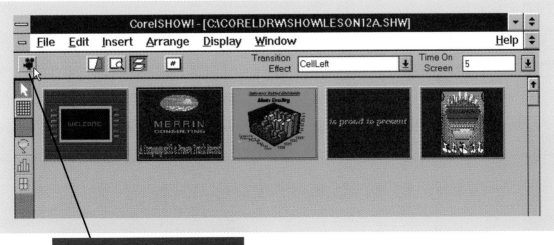

Click here to play the show.

The Generating Slide progress box is displayed. Then you'll be asked if you want to start the screen show.

2. Choose OK.

Selecting Transitions

The way in which the show moves from slide to slide is controlled by the *Transition Effect.* You can select a different transition for each slide (except the animation) to make the presentation more interesting.

1. Click the second slide.

2. Open the Transition Effect list box and click Curtain Open.

3. Click each slide and then choose a Transition Effect from the list box.

4. Click the Screenshow button again, then choose OK to play your show and see the transitions you added.

Setting Presentation Options

The last step in putting together the show is setting some presentation options.

1. Pull down the Display menu and choose Presentation Options.

The Presentation Options dialog box is displayed.

2. Under Timing, select Automatic Advance to next slide.

3. Check Run show continuously until Escape is pressed.

4. Also check Generate slide show in advance.

5. Choose OK.

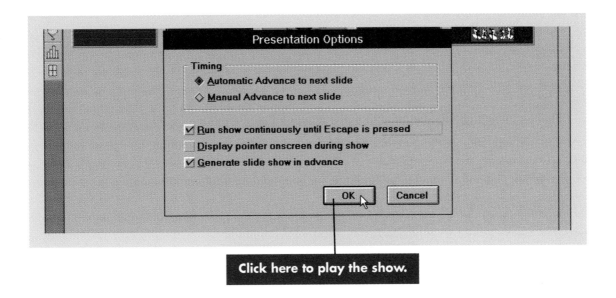

Click here to play the show.

You can play the show by clicking the Screenshow button as you did before. But if you were creating a real show you'd probably do it in advance, save it, and exit CorelSHOW. Then you'd restart CorelSHOW later and start the show. So, do that now.

1. Pull down the File menu and choose Save.

2. Pull down the File menu again and choose Exit.

Playing the Show

To play the show at a later time, follow these steps (but try them now):

1. Start CorelSHOW by double-clicking the CorelSHOW icon.

2. In the Welcome to CorelSHOW dialog box, select Open an Existing Presentation, then choose OK.

3. In the File Name list box, click **lesson09.shw**.

4. Click OK.

5. Once the file is open, click the Screenshow button, then click OK.

6. Press Esc whenever you want to stop the show.

10

Charting with CorelCHART

In the previous lesson, you included a Corel-CHART chart in a CorelSHOW presentation. In this lesson, you'll have an opportunity to learn the basics of CorelCHART while creating your first chart. You'll work with data you enter directly into Corel-CHART's Data Manager and create a pie chart with the data you enter.

Getting Started

The Corel Graphics group window contains the program icons that let you start the Corel applications. This is the same window from which you launched CorelDRAW, CorelSHOW and CorelPAINT.

1. If the Corel Graphics group window is not open, double-click the Corel Graphics icon at the bottom of the Program Manager window.

2. To start CorelCHART, double-click the CorelCHART icon in the Corel Graphics group window.

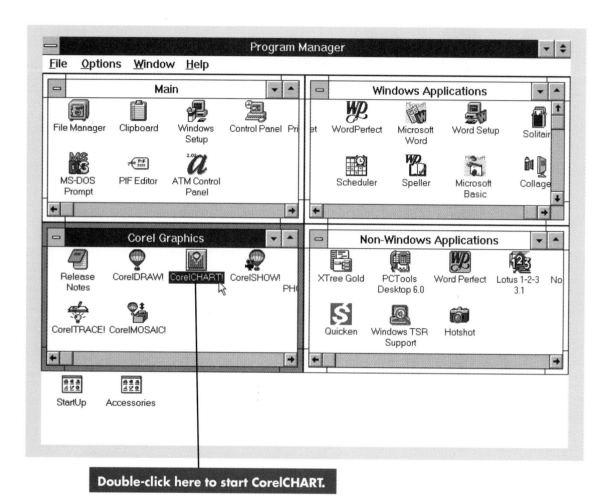

Double-click here to start CorelCHART.

You'll see the CorelCHART Application window. Only one menu is available when CorelCHART is launched.

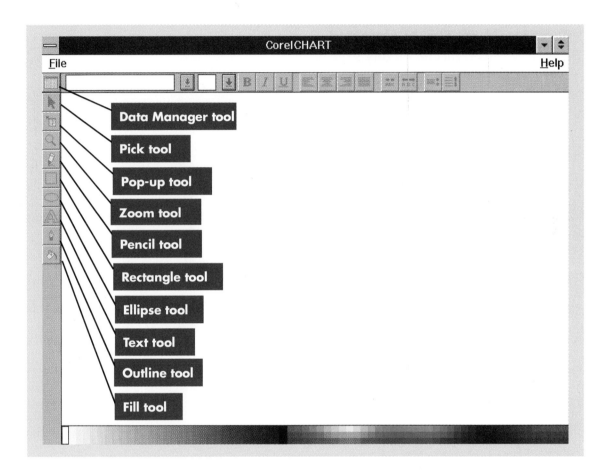

Some of the tools are the same as those found in CorelDRAW, although they do not provide identical flyout menus or functionality. The Data Manager tool at the top of the tool bar lets you switch back and forth between the chart and the spreadsheet on which the chart is based. The Pop-up tool lets you access context-sensitive menus by clicking on part of a chart. You'll notice some differences in the Pick, Zoom, Pencil, Rectangle, Ellipse, and Text tools as you begin to use them.

Creating a New Chart

To begin, you'll create and modify a pie chart.

1. Pull down the File menu and choose New.

The New dialog box is displayed.

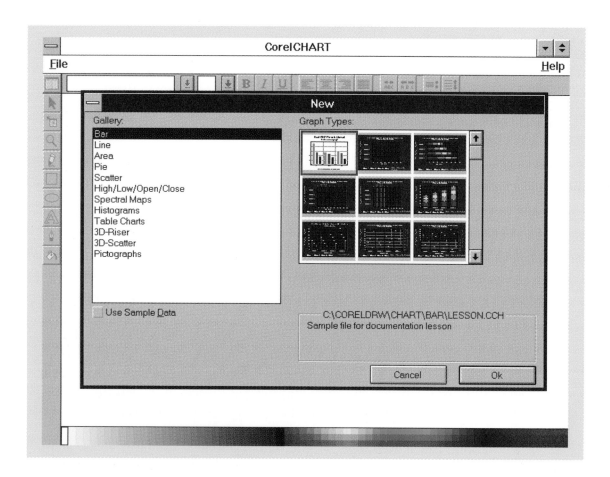

2. In the Gallery list box, click Pie.

Five thumbnails are shown in the Graph Types display box on the right. The first one is selected and its name and description are shown in the box below.

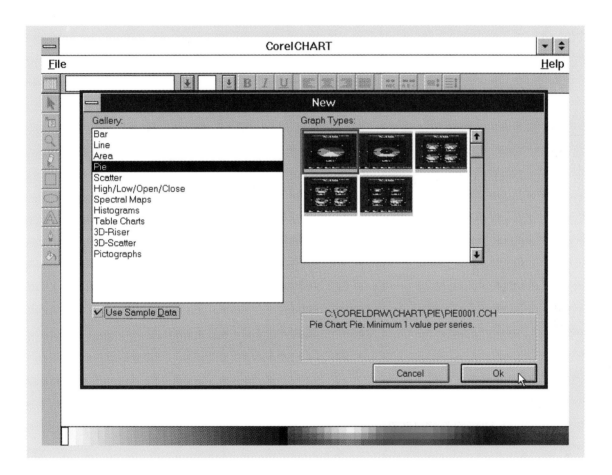

3. Check Use Sample Data.

This will let you see (in your first chart) the relationship between the data in the pie chart and the data in the spreadsheet.

4. Choose OK.

The chart you selected is displayed. Sample data has been used to create the chart.

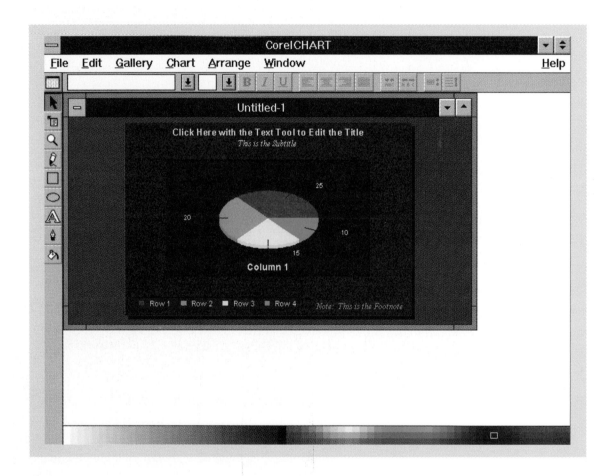

5. Pull down the File menu and choose Save.

The Save Chart dialog box is displayed.

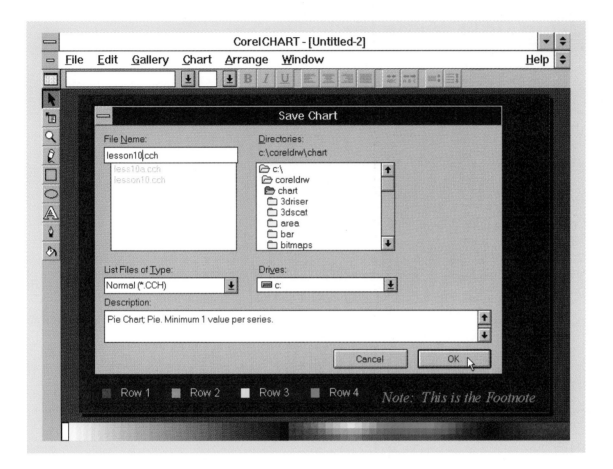

6. In the File Name box, enter **lesson10.cch**.

7. Choose OK.

Now make modifications to the chart by changing the data.

● Note You may want to skip ahead to the end of the lesson to see the finished chart before you begin making the changes.

Using Data Manager

1. Click the Data Manager tool to display CorelCHART's Data Manager.

The Data Manager is where you'll enter the text and numbers on which the chart will be based. If you've worked with any other spreadsheet, you'll have no trouble entering data here.

2. Click in cell A1.

The cursor, which has a dark outline, is in cell A1. Its contents are shown in the Contents box.

3. Type **What's Quick, What's Easy** and press ↵.

The cursor is in cell A2 and its contents are shown in the Contents box.

4. Type **A Matter of Opinion** and press ↵.

The cursor is in cell A3 and its contents are shown in the Contents box.

5. Click before the word **This** and press **Del** until only the word **Note:** remains.

6. Type **Not a scientific survey** and press ↵.

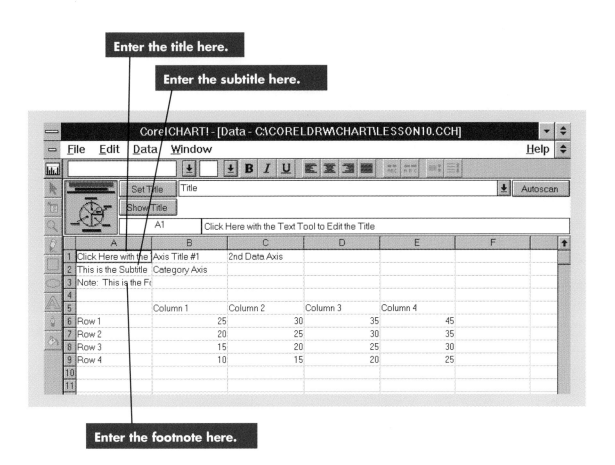

Enter the title here.

Enter the subtitle here.

Enter the footnote here.

You've now entered the title, subtitle, and a footnote for the chart.

Modifying Entries

Now enter the labels for the pie segments.

Quick&Easy

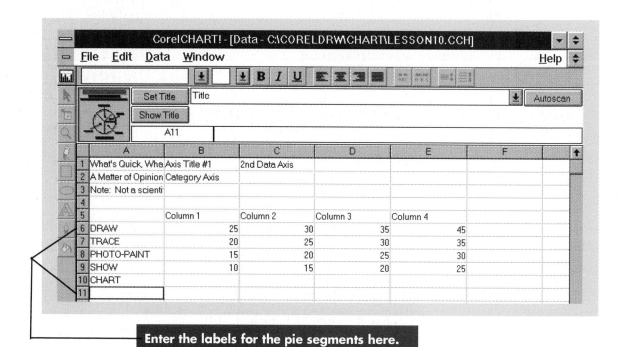

Enter the labels for the pie segments here.

1. Press ↓ twice to move the cursor to cell A6, the first cell tagged as a row header.

2. Type **DRAW** and press ↵.

3. Repeat step 3 to change the row headers to **TRACE**, **PHOTO-PAINT**, and **SHOW**.

4. Add the row header **CHART** to cell A10.

Now let's change and add some data to the spreadsheet.

1. Click cell B6.

To move the cursor to any cell, you can either use the ↑, ↓, ←, or → keys or just click on the cell.

2. Now type 35.

3. Change the number in cell B7 to 25.

4. Change the number in cell B9 to 15.

5. Add the number 10 to cell B10.

The sample data in the spreadsheet includes some data we don't need for a pie chart, so let's delete it.

1. Move the cursor to cell B1.

2. Press Del.

3. Move the cursor to cell B2 and press Del.

4. Move the cursor to cell C1 and press Del.

Now delete a block of data.

5. Click in cell C5, then press Shift and click in cell E9.

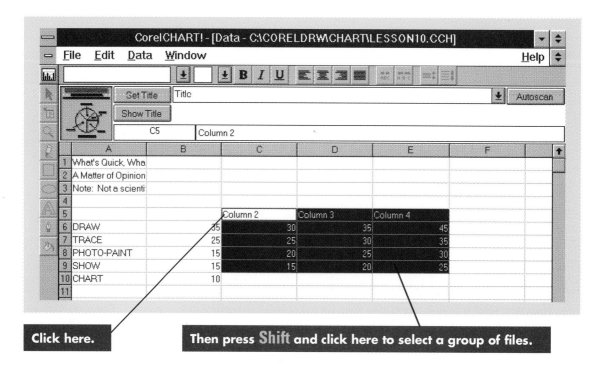

Click here.

Then press Shift and click here to select a group of files.

6. Pull down the Edit menu and choose Clear.

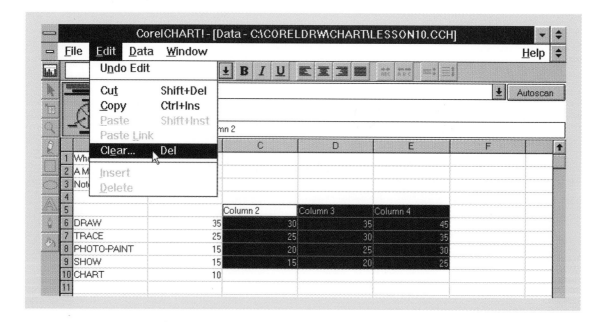

7. Select and delete any numbers or text left in your chart that
you don't see in the next screen illustration.

Identifying Chart Data

Now we'll have to identify the new information we added to the chart
so CorelCHART knows what to do with it. This is called *tagging*.

1. Click in cell A6, then press Shift and click in cell A10.

2. Click the prompt button to open the Tag list box.

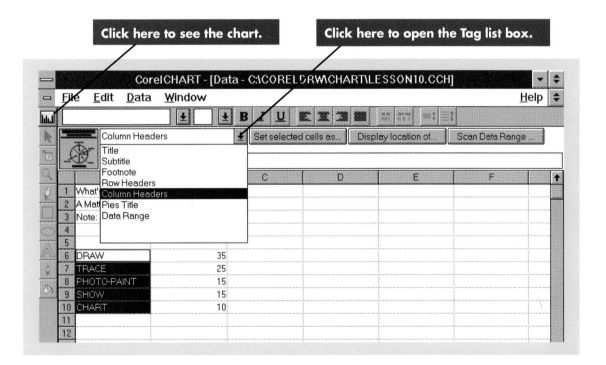

3. Click Column Headers.

4. Click the Set Column Headers button.

5. Click in cell B6, then press Shift and click in cell B10.

6. Click the prompt button to open the Tag list box again.

7. Click Data Range.

8. Click the Set Data Range button.

When you work with sample data, you are also working with data that is already tagged, or identified to CorelCHART. If you change the contents of a cell, the cell is still tagged, so you do not have to tag it again. You changed the contents of the cells tagged as Title, Subtitle, and Footnote, but want those cells used in the same way, so you do not have to tag them again.

However, when you add data to a cell that is not tagged, you need to tag that cell. You also need to retag a group of cells when you add one or more cells with the same tag. For example, when you add cells to the data range, you need to select all the cells in the data range and set the selected cells as the data range.

Now that you have all your data entered and tagged, go back and see how your chart looks so far.

Modifying a Chart

1. Click the Chart View tool to see the chart.

When you are working in Data Manager, the Chart View tool is the first tool.

The chart you just created is displayed. Now, you can modify the way the chart looks using CorelCHART's tools.

2. Click the maximize button in the upper right of the chart window to make the best use of your viewing space.

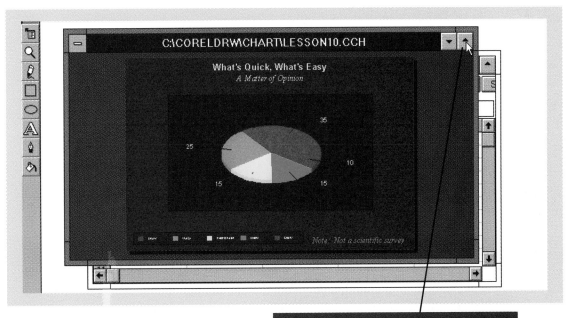

Click here to maximize the window.

3. Click the Pick tool if it is not selected, then click anywhere on the chart background.

4. Open the Fill flyout and choose the Custom Colors tool.

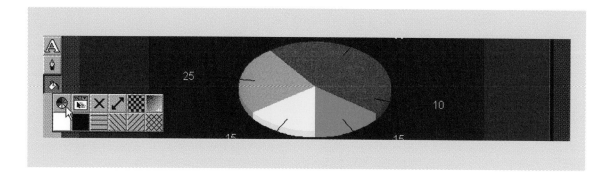

The Color dialog box is displayed.

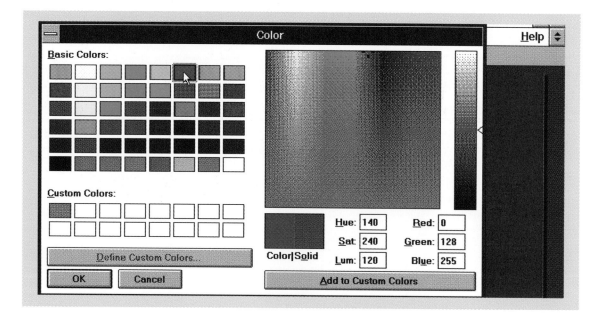

5. Click on one of the lighter colors.

6. Choose OK.

7. Click the page frame, then repeat steps 4 through 6 to
change the frame color.

Enhancing Chart Text

Now let's modify the text.

1. Click the Pick tool, then click anywhere on the chart title.

The chart title is surrounded by a selection box.

2. In the Ribbon, open the Typeface list box by clicking the prompt button, then click a different typeface.

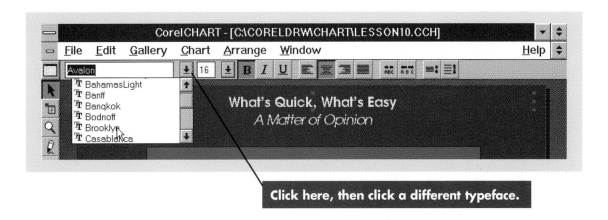

Click here, then click a different typeface.

3. Open the Point size list box by clicking the prompt button, then click a larger point size.

4. Click the Bold button.

5. Click on a color in the color palette to change the color of the text so it stands out against the background.

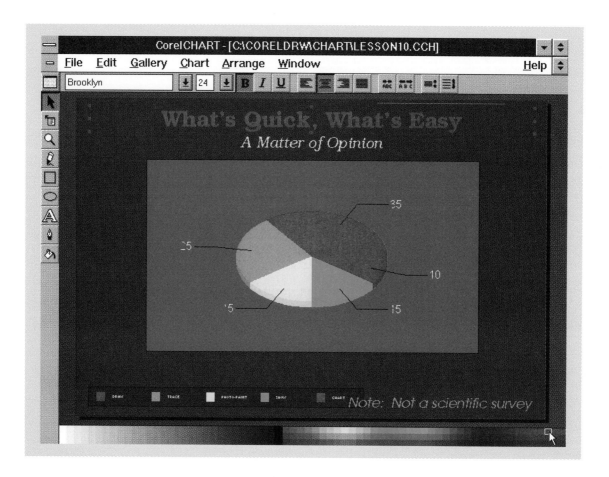

6. Repeat steps 1 through 5 to change the characteristics of the subtitle.

7. Select the footnote at the bottom of the page and change its characteristics as well.

8. While you have the footnote selected, drag the left side of the selection box to the right, so it does not stretch across the entire page.

Drag from here to here.

Selecting Chart Colors

Now change the colors used in the pie.

1. With the Pick tool still selected, click on a pie slice.

The slice is outlined in a contrasting color.

2. Click any color in the color palette.

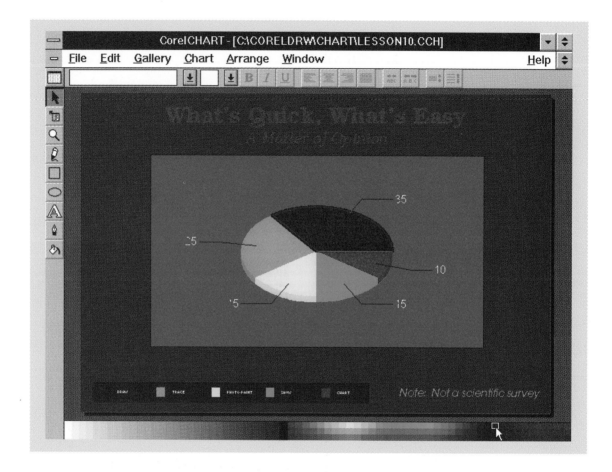

3. Click the next pie segment and change the color by clicking in the color palette.

4. Repeat the steps until you are satisfied with all the colors used in the pie.

Modifying the Legend

You'll notice that as you change the colors, the colors in the pie legend also change. Let's change the way the legend is displayed.

1. Click the Pop-up tool.

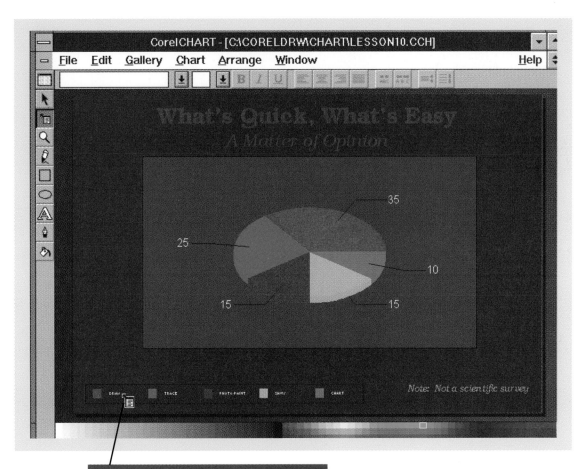

Point and click with the Pop-up tool.

2. Click the word DRAW.

The Row Header pop-up menu is displayed.

3. Click Legend.

Click here.

The Legend dialog box is displayed.

4. Click on Autofit Legend Text so it is not checked.

5. Select Text on Marker.

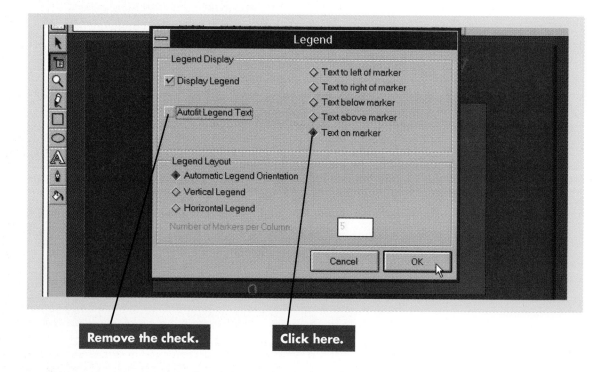

Remove the check.

Click here.

6. Choose OK.

7. Click the first square on the left.

The Row Header pop-up menu is displayed again.

8. Click Marker Shape.

A list box with marker shapes is displayed. You can scroll the list with ↓ to view each shape.

9. Click Circle.

10. Click each square, then change it to a circle.

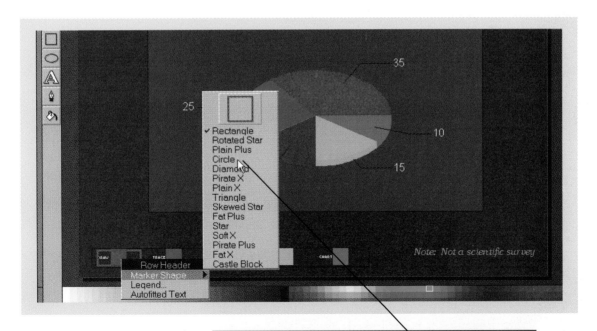

Click here to change the marker shape to a circle.

You may have noticed that even though you selected Text on Marker, the text is to the left. That's because of the text justification that was set, so let's fix that. First, let's increase the viewing size of the chart.

1. Click the Zoom tool, then click the 200% tool.

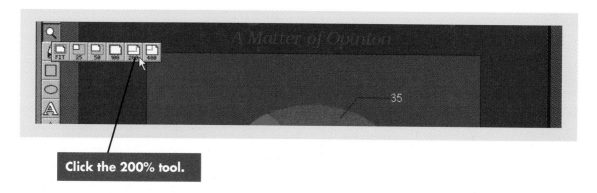

Click the 200% tool.

2. Use the scroll bars to display the legend.

Drag here to display the legend.

3. With the Pick tool selected, click **DRAW**.

It's surrounded by a highlighting box. In the Ribbon, you'll see that the Left justification button is depressed.

4. Click the Center justification button.

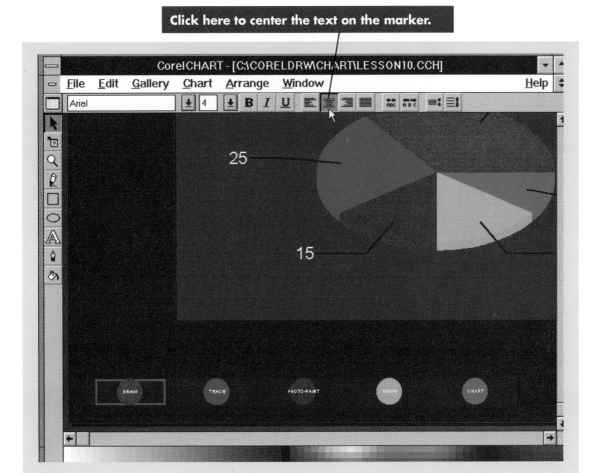

Click here to center the text on the marker.

All the words in the legend are centered over the colors that represent them. Let's change the legend a bit more.

5. Click the rectangle background behind the legend.

6. Open the Fill flyout and choose the No fill tool.

Quick & Easy

Click here to remove the background.

7. Open the Outline flyout and choose No outline.

Click here to remove the outline.

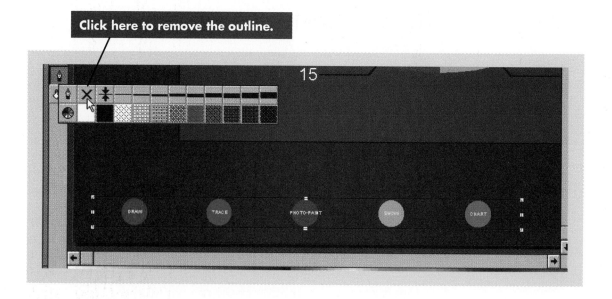

8. Drag the legend so it overlaps the bottom of the chart frame as in the illustration.

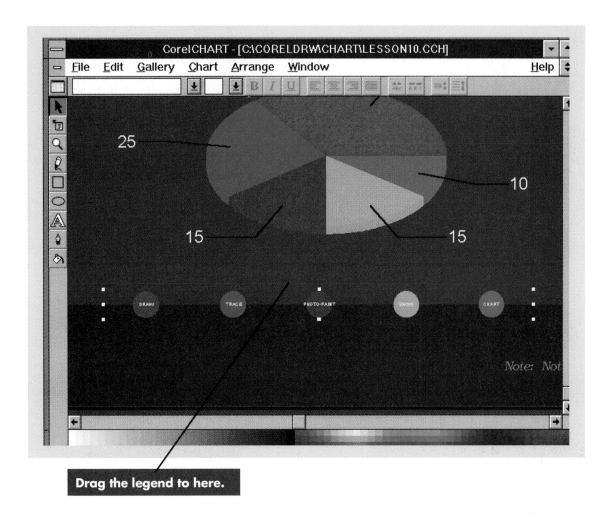

Drag the legend to here.

Finishing Touches

The pie chart might look more interesting if you make a few more changes.

1. Click the Zoom tool, then click the 100% tool so you can see the whole chart again.

2. Click the Pop-up tool.

3. Click the largest pie slice.

The Pie Slice pop-up menu is displayed.

4. Click Detach Slice.

5. Click Default.

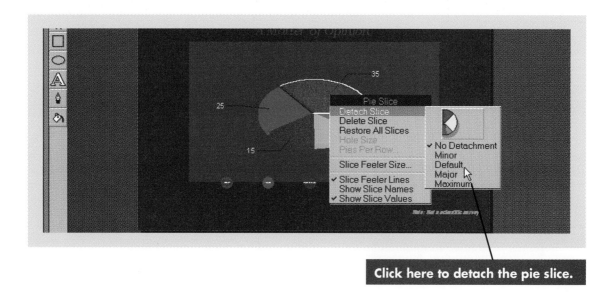

Click here to detach the pie slice.

6. Click the rectangle background behind the chart.

The Pie Chart Frame pop-up menu is displayed.

7. Click Pie Thickness.

8. Click Major.

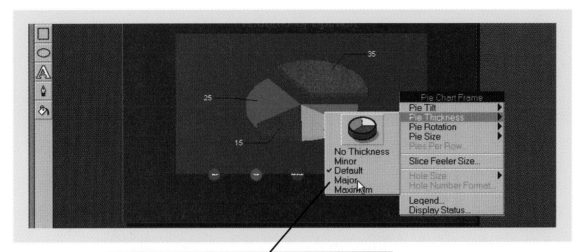

Click here to give the pie slice more depth.

You may want to change the way the numbers look, or any of the colors or text in the chart. Our finished chart is on the next page. Before you finish this lesson, don't forget to save your chart.

1. Pull down the File menu and choose Save.

2. Pull down the File menu again and choose Close.

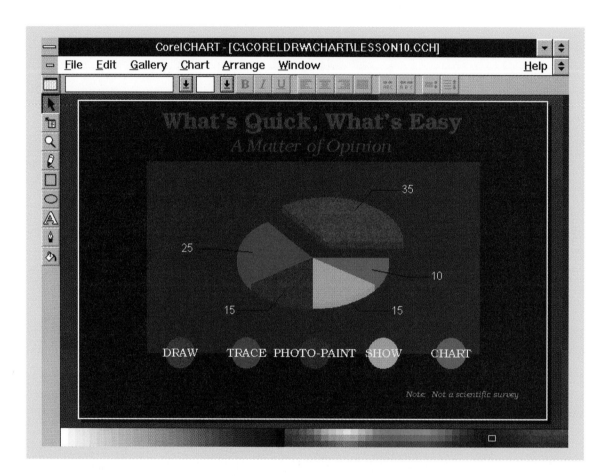

Where Do I Go
From Here?

In the course of reading and using this book, you've learned a great deal about CorelDRAW techniques and features, and have even acquired basic skills with the CorelCHART, Corel-SHOW, and CorelPHOTO-PAINT auxiliary programs. You have a firm grasp on the essentials, but since CorelDRAW is such a powerful program, you'll probably want to learn about its other capabilities at some point. For example, you might want to learn how to import and export graphic files, taking advantage of CorelDRAW's numerous filters; how to manipulate type and text and use fills; how to integrate your graphics with desktop publishing; how to use output service bureaus; or how to fine-tune CorelDRAW.

If you'd like to start with a beginner's tutorial that lets you try things out step-by-step and then use a quick, practical reference that answers your questions as they come up, then *CorelDRAW 3 Running Start*, Len Gilbert, SYBEX, 1993, is the right book for you. It covers the material in this book with a little more explanation and explores new areas as well; at the same time, it has a handy reference section in the second half of the book.

If you think you're ready for a how-to book that doubles as a reference and covers CorelDRAW in depth, try *Mastering CorelDRAW 3*, Steve Rimmer, SYBEX, 1992. It's full of great examples and hands-on steps, and it explains everything from the most basic topics to the most advanced.

If you'd like a quick reference book to answer occasional questions, then you want *CorelDRAW 3 Instant Reference*, Gordon Padwick, SYBEX, 1992.

INDEX

●

This index contains certain typographical conventions to assist you in finding information. **Boldface** page numbers are references to primary topics and explanations that are emphasized in the text. Roman page numbers are standard references. *Italics* indicate page numbers that reference figures.

W

Welcome to CorelSHOW dialog box, 187–188, *188*, 216

whales, clip art for, 80

width
of brushes, 175–177
of lines, 183

Width and Shape Workbox, 163, *163*, 177

Windows requirements, **3–4**

Z

Zoom In tool, 63, *63*

Zoom menu, 62, *63*

Zoom tool, *21*, 62, 171–172, *172*, 219, *219*

zooming
in charts, 219, *219*
in paintings, **171–172**
text, **62–65**, **105–107**

ZSoftImage files, 184